Turning your *heart* to *God* is the key to living victoriously. In this study, you will explore how to **know** you are walking with God. You will learn to evaluate your spiritual condition at any time.

Having your heart fixed on Jesus is imperative to knowing and believing HOW deeply God loves you. Accepting the fact that God loves you with unchanging love, changes everything (1 John 4:16-19). In love, God the Father gave His Son, Jesus, to Redeem you for His Highest Purpose, which is Jesus' glory. You will study about God's Highest Purpose and how you significantly fit into His plan.

Once you know and believe Jesus loves you and accept that He alone is your righteousness, thus you are complete in Him concerning salvation, your heart overflows with gratitude and love for Him. The more you learn to focus on who Jesus is to you personally, the more you grow in loving Him, thus, the more you turn your heart to Him. In Jesus you find your greatest purpose in life now and forever.

Jesus died as a substitute in our place and now lives and makes us acceptable to His Father, and that is 100% by His own, perfect righteousness.

Get this down now and get it down big: Jesus is Everything to God the Father and by loving Him, you find He is Everything you need and must have for significance in life.

The most important thing is fellowship with Jesus in a love-driven relationship, where you strive to be fully surrendered to Him as your greatest treasure. Never settle for serving Jesus out of obligation, duty, necessity or for any other reason than the fact that He loves you and you love Him. Love-driven obedience is God's goal for you. Anything else will not result in fulfilment and significance in your life.

Throughout God's Word He called individuals and His people corporately to accomplish things much "bigger" than their strengths, skills and abilities. Therefore, they had to function in faith (depending fully on Him) to do His will. God's will has more to do with what He is doing in you than it does the things He wants to do through you.

As you journey through this book, you may ask, *"Why haven't we understood about the heart before now?"* According to God's Word, when His people depart from Him in their hearts, He simply sends spiritual blindness and they cannot see the depth of their errors. Such blindness of hearts causes them all sorts of confusion, defeat, and problems. When people willfully live in ways that displease Him (which happens when their hearts are turned away from Him) He removes protection from their minds, which results in spiritual blindness. People without a heart toward God entangle themselves in the world by making poor decisions which lead to bondage to all sorts of things.

To gain the most from this study, it is best to give yourself plenty of time to think about what you are learning. When you sacrifice to gain insight from God's Word, He honors you with deeper insights. Sacrifice to spend time with Jesus as you study. Such as, get up earlier or spend less time doing un necessary things. Make it your goal to have intimate encounters with Him. Concentrate on loving and seeking Him as your primary goal and your life will be enriched.

Just a few weeks of devoted interaction with Jesus in His Word can change one's life forever. So, get ready to be challenged, changed and to freshly join God in His work in your life and world.

Seeing God is showing us how to live more rightly related to Him and how to be victorious over the world, the flesh, and the devil, what does this reveal? It reveals He is turning our hearts back to Himself for revival (spiritual renewal).

 Notes: Memory Verse Clip Art provided by WordPerfect, Corel Corporation.

Larry White
6 Iroquois Dr.
Cherokee Village, AR 72529
e-mail: LWW72529@yahoo.com

A principle I am seeking to learn, is to ask myself one primary, two-part question in every situation I find myself, whether good and bad. It is, "God, what are you saying to me in this and how do you want me to respond?" These are what matter the most.

Pause and Pray each of the following:
1. Thank God for a blessing in your life of which you are extremely grateful.
2. Ask Him to meet a special need in your life.
3. Pray for Revival and Spiritual Awakening in America.
4. Pray for everyone who will study this book.

THANKS:

To my wife, Angie, I am deeply grateful for her love and patience as I have spent so much time in ministry, study and writing.

To the memory of my dad, Edwin L. White Sr., who taught me to love and respect God's Holy and perfect Word.

To Dr. Winfred P. Bridges, I am grateful for his help in editing the early edition of this book. He is a gifted, special friend and brother.

To the family of faith in Calvary Baptist Church, Harrisburg, AR, where God allowed me to write the first edition of this book.

To my family of faith in First Baptist Church, Cherokee Village, AR, who graciously gave support and allowed me to have time to study, write and prepare this work for publishing.

To Louann Street, a dear sister, for her investment in this project. She worked with me for several weeks proofreading and giving suggestions that have greatly enhanced this writing.

Contents:

Forward 1
Acknowledgments 2
Contents 3
Introduction: My Journey to Life and Freedom... 4
How to Know God's Will... 8

Week One: Walking with God and Understanding Your Heart.
Day One: **God Sees Your Heart.** 11
Day Two: **God gives "A New Heart"**.. 14
Day Three: **Living and Loving Effectively by Giving All to Jesus** 16
Day Four: **A Heart Ready to Turn at Any Point** 19
Day Five: **A Man after God's Heart** 21
    (Church Ministry and My Journey to Freedom, p. 23)

Week Two: Gaining Freedom over Temptation and Sin's Power.
Day One: **God and His Word are in Your Heart** 28
Day Two: **A Call to Full Surrender** 32
Day Three: **Surrender is a Continual Process** 36
Day Four: **God Made You for Himself**.. 39
Day Five: **You are Free in Jesus to Obey His Will** 42
    (My Journey with Anger and Freedom in Christ, p. 43)

Week Three: Keeping Your Heart on God.
Day One: **Living a Changed Life** 48
Day Two: **Don't Confuse Forgiving Others with Reconciliation** 50
Day Three: **Living for God's High Purpose**.. 53
Day Four: **Prayer and God's High Purpose** 56
Day Five: **God's High Purpose and Loving Others** 59
    (A Young Man and His Journey, p. 60)

Week Four: Where Jesus Leads, I will Walk with Him with All of My Heart.
Day One: **Defeating Temptation Takes Place in Your Mind**................................. 62
Day Two: **Walking Joyfully with Jesus?**... 65
Day Three: **Revival and Your Walk with Jesus** 68
Day Four: **Walking with Jesus in Obedience for His Glory** 71
Day Five: **What is in Your Eye**.. 74
    (My Journey and a Struggle to Forgive, p. 76)

Week Five: Walking with God and Learning More about Him.
Day One: **God Comforts His Hurting Children** 79
Day Two: **An Example of Faithfulness During Severe Adversity** 82
Day Three: **An Example of Unfaithfulness During Severe Adversity** 85
Day Four: **A Proper Knowledge of God** 88
Day Five: **Increasing in the Knowledge of God Yields Many Rewards** 91
    (My Journey and Learning More About How God Works with Us, Always Torn, p.92)

Week Six: Subjection to Authority: God's Way to Greatness.
Day One: **God is in Control of All that Happens to You** 96
Day Two: **Avoiding a Wrestling Match that You Can't Win** 99
Day Three: **Winning an Important Decision in God's Court** 102
Day Four: **Sometimes Doing Right Results in Suffering** 107
Day Five: **Believers are Required to Obey the Laws of Our Land** 111
    (My Journey and a Sobering Truth, p. 114)

Scripture References 116
  Endnotes.. 117

My Journey to Life and Freedom

To help you understand my perspective from which this book was written, it is necessary to share some things about my life.

Some of the things I will share have been very difficult for me. It has taken me almost a lifetime to face these painful issues. If I did not think it would help many who need to know God can help, I would not share the following. Yet, unless I share about my life, many working through this study may think, "There is no way this writer can understand my pain." Some might think I was reared in a perfect home without any tragic events, but this was not the case. First, understand there are no perfect homes, just some better than others.

I have received permission from my mother and three eldest siblings to share this information. Because the three eldest were much more personally involved in the life-altering events that brought Jesus into my life, I felt it necessary to seek their approval.

My purpose for sharing is to help you know God is also able to help you. I have no purpose of putting anyone in a bad light. My family members are some of the most special people in the world. Each one is so unique. God has taught me many wonderful things about Himself through them. But, I must share a few things that are not very pleasant. Dad gave me permission to share these things many years before his death.

I was reared in a small farming community in Northeast Arkansas (Heafer, [hay fer]). I was the sixth child in a family of seven, consisting of five girls and two boys. Dad was a hard worker, working long hours on the farm. He was a great farmer.

I was strongly willed and a very difficult child. No one seemed to be able to control me. I always felt I could outsmart or outlast anyone. The three oldest children were girls. The second born, Linda, was special. My only brother is four years older than I and four years younger than her. When I came along as a baby boy in the midst of mostly girls, I suppose her age and temperament bonded us together.

Mom was often very sick during my early years, so Linda and my eldest sister were kind of an extra support for me. They were the ones I could talk to. Linda was sixteen in October of my eighth year.

On New Year's Eve, a tragic event took place. Linda was raped. Our home life had become very difficult even before this horrible tragedy. Dad, whom I loved as much as anyone on earth, had struggled with alcohol for several years. After that night, everything changed for all of us. This sister whom I knew loved me, suddenly had no time for me. All she wanted to do was cry and be alone. I did not understand. I thought somehow I had done something to cause her to reject me. It seemed everyone would tell me to leave her alone.

Things degenerated very quickly in our home. Linda tried to go back to high school, but could not face her peers. My life seemed as though it was coming apart at the seams. Four months later, April 9th, Linda took her life. She and Mom were at home that day while we were at school. Mom heard the gunshot and went in and found Linda. When Mom and Linda were found two hours later by our sister just younger than Linda, Mom had suffered a complete nervous breakdown. For the next six years, I practically lost my mom. She was in and out of hospitals and struggled to face reality.

When I was fourteen, she began to make great strides in improvement. She would do things for us that seemed like she wanted to go the extra mile. Dad told me to let her do anything she wanted to do because he felt she was seeking to make up for lost time.

Soon after Linda's death (a week or so), Dad took us to church. He turned his heart to the Lord that day and was a changed man. When the invitation was given that Sunday, Dad started out into the aisle and dropped to his knees. He crawled to the altar in front of the church crying out for forgiveness. Several have shared with me how that day had a dramatic impact upon their lives.

Not long after that (August) I was saved. After a few years, Dad became a leader in that church. He developed a love for the Word of God more than anyone I have known. On rainy days and during the winter months, he would often study for hours, if not all day. Every morning when I got up to get ready for school or go to work, he would be at the breakfast table studying his Bible. He could quote large passages of scripture. He loved to talk about God and His Word. He would witness and share with anyone who would stand still and many times when they were trying to get away.

Although I was saved that year, I continued to struggle with the changes in our home. I just didn't know what was going on and we didn't talk about it. In a few short years, I became angry and resentful over the things that were coming to light. At the age of eleven, I discovered what the word "rape" meant. The more I discovered, the more angry and resentful I became. I felt I had been cheated by that rapist.

Tragic events, such as those Linda went through, have horrible effects upon a family. I became more difficult to control. My anger almost destroyed me and I hurt many people. Everyone in authority over me, seemingly, became my enemy. I refused to submit to anyone. Dad told me (after I was grown) that he whipped me more than all of the other six children combined. He said, "At one time I thought there was no hope for you."

At the age of twenty, God called me to preach. A few weeks later, I married Angie Merrell. I met Angie in the church where I grew up. The day we met, I was sitting near the back of the auditorium. I wasn't paying attention to the preacher. I was talking to a friend when I glanced back and saw her (she was seated one row behind me). When we made eye contact she said, "Why don't you shut up?" I said to my friend so she could hear me, "Who is that crazy girl?" A few weeks later we started dating. We dated for about three years.

After a few years of farming with Dad and serving as bi-vocational pastor of a small church, Dad shared some personal things with me.

One day just before sunset Dad told me he needed to tell me something. We sat down and he said, "Son, I know God is really going to use your life. I feel I need to share some things with you." He started to cry. Dad did not cry easily. I sat and listened. He said, "When you were a child, just before your sister was raped, God dealt with me about getting right with Him and going back to church. It was the first year that I was self-employed, and I didn't think I could afford to take off work every Sunday.

The Sunday School Superintendent and the pastor came to see me and God convicted me so strongly, but I resisted Him." Dad went on to say, "One other night, God dealt with me in a powerful way. His voice could not have been more real had He spoken aloud." He said, "Sitting there, I clearly made a decision in my heart. I said, 'NO' to God. I told God, 'I have seven children and a sick wife, I have to work whenever I can.'" And, he did work seven days a week most of the time. He said, "The conviction immediately changed. It scared me, but I felt I just couldn't change. It was later that week when your sister was raped." He went on to say, "Within four months, one of the busiest times of the year, planting season, I had lost a daughter and practically my wife." He said, "It was not long before I felt I had lost control of most of all I had."

He said, "What I had told God was most important to me, my family, He used to deal with me." He said, "Son, God dealt with me as a son because I was saved when I was twelve years old and I know it." He went on to say, "I want you to know these things because I feel like you will need this someday."

A few years later, while I was trying to work through the anger inside of me, we talked about these things again. I asked him if I could share with others the things he had shared with me. He assured me I could and that was the reason he had told me those things. He said, "If the Lord can use you to warn others and keep them from going through what we all have gone through, I want you to do it."

Dear friend, I don't know what you have gone through in your life, but I know God has a purpose for all He has allowed. What the enemy has sought to destroy us with, God wants to use to bring us to the end of ourselves so our trust is only in Him.

The most painful and troubling things of our lives can become a launching pad for God's greatest work in and through us, IF, we will turn our hearts and surrender our lives to Him.

In 1982, I left the farming business and moved toward a full-time work as a pastor. I wanted to be used of God. I wanted to see Him work and exalt His name in and through me. I wanted to be "All His" and that is my quest today.

I really thought I had worked through most of my anger problem earlier in my preaching years. I had come a long way, but freedom from anger was not mine. I was a lot better, but continued to be ruled by frustration and inward turmoil.

I will share about two sides of my life. First, I will share about the closing years of Dad's life. Later, I'll share about the last fourteen years of church ministry (up to 1997). God used both of these to break and prepare me to begin my journey of seeking Him with all of my heart.

In November of 1989, Dad suffered a serious stroke. He was left unable to do anything for himself. He could not talk, swallow, or move, except for his left leg and arm. He was totally at the mercy of his care givers. I made some decisions about his health that for the next seven years would tear my heart out. Prior to the major strokes, Dad had several mini-strokes. He asked me to be very much involved in his and Mom's future financial and medical decisions if things came to where he could not make those decisions.

I will never forget the day I stood in the parsonage driveway and promised him that I would not allow him to be placed on unnecessary life-support, nor would I allow him to be placed in a nursing home.

A couple of months later he suffered the major stroke. A doctor, who is a good friend, gave his opinion to me. He was quite sure Dad would not live more than three months, or six at the longest. I allowed some things to be done that apparently Dad did not want. My wife and I took Dad home to live with us. This same doctor pled with me not to do it. He said a nursing home was the only option for someone in his condition.

After a couple of weeks and many sleepless nights, I came home from work to see my wife standing in the doorway of his room completely exhausted. She looked as though she was about to hit the floor. I thought, "I cannot continue to do this to her." I felt like my world had closed in on me. There was no good solution. I called the nursing home in our town and they said, "Bring him down." When I told Dad what I had to do, he began to groan and cry (because he could not speak). He looked at me with a very disturbing look. I'll never forget it.

Later that day, we took him to the nursing home. I left while the workers prepared the room for his condition. After awhile, I returned. Dad took his left hand and jerked the feeding tube from his stomach. He stared sternly at me. I broke down and began to cry. I met the nurse in the hall. I pointed to his room. She ran in and after a struggle they fixed the tube.

I tried to explain to him why I did what I felt I had to do. He would only look at me with disappointment and cry. The nurse assured me that he did not know what he was doing. But, I knew he did. They finally restrained his arm, after he had destroyed several tubes. Dad soon learned there was no use fighting.

Dad lived for seven years like that. I spent days and weeks in and out of the hospital with him. I would visit as often as I was able to handle it. Many nights I would go by and visit him after a meeting at church. I would leave there and drive around through the hills near our home and cry out to God. I spent hours doing this. I would park in the country and cry and pray. I would cry at church while preaching. I would cry at night. I would dream Dad regained his voice and we would laugh and talk and he assured me he understood. Then I would awake and realize it was only a dream. I know I dreamed this same dream more than one hundred times during that seven years.

During those seven years, I was brought to the end of many personal ambitions and goals. I learned a lot about the shortness of life. I learned the most important things are Jesus and the people He has placed in my life. I saw how I had spent much of my life on things which have no lasting value.

For seven years, November 1989- November 1996, I lived as it seemed on the edge of life, just hanging on by a thread. Many times I felt I could not face another day. I was just trying to make it through each day. Without a doubt, it was Jesus who brought me through. The faith that I was taught to have in Him was all that seemed to have remained.

I am grateful you are taking time to read this book. I hope this introduction will help you as you consider each lesson. These lessons were not written to preach or teach. They came from my personal journal as I sought God while going through the trials mentioned above.

Dad was used of God to teach me His Word while he had his health. When his health failed, God used him in silence to teach me a lot of practical applications of the Word that He wanted me to learn.

As I write this testimony today, June 9, 1997 (my son's birthday), I stand amazed at the great God I serve. Dad died last November (1996).

As I revise this book (the winter of 2017- the summer of 2018) I am rejoicing over the opportunity to be involved in this ministry. My family has now lost both parents in death. Mom died on Mother's Day, May 9, 1999.

Before her death, God blessed me in a special way by allowing me to visit her before Sunday School that morning. My wife, Angie, had suggested that we visit Mom early, rather than in the afternoon. We had never done that before, but I felt it was a good idea.

We took Mom some roses and had a good visit. She wasn't feeling very well. I asked her if I could take her to the hospital, but she refused to go. She said, "I just want to stay here and rest."

At ten minutes after twelve, Mom's heart stopped. We were in the parking lot at church when she died. The nurse called and I went there immediately. Had we not gone that morning, I would have missed that special time with her. I thank God for putting that thought in Angie's heart.

This work is dedicated in the loving memory of
Linda Sue White,
Gertrude White (Mom)
&
Edwin L. C. White Sr.

It is very important to allow the pressures and struggles of our lives to rend and break our hearts, because God says in Psalm 34:8, "**The Lord is nigh unto them that are of a broken heart; and saveth such as be of a contrite spirit.**"

It is recognized weaknesses (those things in our lives and minds that we can't change) that can become our greatest platform for being effectiveness in the Christian life.

In our weaknesses, we find Jesus' strength pouring through us. When we move and have our being, while acutely conscious of our insufficiencies in ourselves, we have the opportunity to be powerful weapons in God's hands. This is because our weaknesses humble us and destroy pride, therefore, they keep us more usable in the things that matter the most.

I especially encourage pastors and church leaders to allow the pressures you feel in ministry, your family and others you love, to take you to a fresh surrender of your life and heart to Jesus for His glory.

The following article speaks to Knowing and Doing God's Will and how your heart is part of that process.

How to Know God's Will.

Romans 12:1 **I beseech you therefore, brethren, by the mercies of God, that ye <u>present</u> your bodies a living sacrifice, holy, acceptable unto God, which is your reasonable service. 2 And be not conformed to this world: but be ye transformed by the renewing of your mind, that ye may prove what is that good, and acceptable, and perfect, <u>will of God</u>.**

Point of Truth: To not miss the very best of God's will, you must be striving to be surrendered to Him. Your surrender is to be based on a love-relationship with Jesus, thus, you are love-driven to do His will.

The more you grow in knowing God's purpose for His people and how you fit into that plan, the more you desire to love Him and fulfill His purpose for your life.

The goal of this book is to help you become (if you are not) so intensely focused on Jesus Christ that you find yourself in the center of His will with your heart striving to be humbly and fully surrendered to Him.

It is God's responsibility to communicate His will to His people. A dad would never tell his child to do his will and not tell that child what his will is, and neither would God.

According to Romans 12:1 the first thing you must do to discover the "**will of God**" is "**present**" your body "**a living sacrifice, ...**" This is more than "doing" something. It is striving to become the person God wants you to be, which is one who lives every moment in a love-driven relationship with Jesus. The Christian life is ALL about "Life with JESUS," which is for His glory and your greatest good.

From a human perspective, your body is the most important part of your earthly life, because what you <u>desire to do and be</u> in your body shows how sacrificially surrendered you are to Jesus.
Point of Truth: The way you are willing to live your life reveals the depth of your sacrificial surrender to Jesus.

What we desire to do in our bodies reflects the depth of our spiritual lives. This is why the first thing God says in the verses above is **present your bodies a living sacrifice** and then He tells what that looks like, **holy, acceptable unto God**.

The first thing in discovering the will of God is to "**PRESENT**" yourself to Him sacrificially. This means having a predetermined willingness to do whatever He wants, even before He tells you what it is, because you trust Him that much. In other words, you are striving to be fully surrendered to Jesus, therefore you are striving to be all His in your heart and mind. I say "striving" because we are always in the process and not yet all we will be when He finishes His work in us. We are works in progress.

This progressive work moves forward in our lives based on where our hearts are given. And where each one's heart is given has much to do with the accurate knowledge he/she has of God and His will. The more we understand His love for us and how being in His will is the greatest place to live, the more we turn our hearts to Him. God says the sacrificial surrender of your life to Him is **reasonable**. Such surrender becomes **reasonable** when you understand the ultimate outcome of your faith in Jesus, which is God's glorious purpose for creating you (we will explore more about this in this study). He created you for Himself. His plan for your life is the best life for you. It is **reasonable** to strive to become the person God made you to be, because it is best life you can ever know.

The right kind of faith in Jesus results in daily walking in heart-to-heart, love-driven fellowship with Him where you know He loves you unconditionally. Everything God wants for us is in Jesus, and we access it all by living for Him in a love-driven relationship, rather than trying to relate to Him out of duty, obligation, necessity, keeping rules or laws, or any other man-pressured purpose.

As we learn to relate to Jesus, based on the fact that He loves us and gave Himself for us to fulfill His great plan in us, we are filled with gratitude, worship and praise to Him.

When you know in your heart that you are striving to be ALL HIS in every way because you love Him, then you can be confident the next point can safely be applied to your life, but only then.

The next point in knowing God's will is "**DESIRE.**" I say this because of the words **be ye transformed by the renewing of your mind** (Romans 12:2) which mean your thinking, your desiring, is in line with God's will. This is exactly what a renewed mind is. A renewed mind is no longer seeking to be **conformed to the world** because you are striving to be sacrificially surrendered to God in every **holy** and **acceptable** way.

There are basically two types of approaches to striving to do God's will. The first is a natural way to think, thus it is LAW-driven. This type of person lives in an atmosphere of forcing oneself to do what is right because of laws, feelings of legal obligation, duty, rules or to avoid guilt, etc.

The second is very different. It is LOVE-driven. It is when you know and believe God loves you unconditionally (1 John 4:16). In response to His love you love Him and show it by you striving to please Him. In your love for God, you strive to do what He wants because you don't want to disappoint Him. This is a heart-to-heart, love-driven relationship, which is exactly what every maturing believer grows to understand. This is a life of intimate relationship with Jesus out of which flows an increasing desire to please Him.

When your desires are toward Jesus and His will, your thinking will reflect it, which will be revealed to you and others by how you strive to live your life in your body. Your body is the proving ground of all that you are in your heart, your wants, desires and goals. When right, your heart is a reflection of the accurate knowledge of God that you have, thus the precise understanding of His ultimate purpose for your life, which is to be a glorious trophy of His grace, and that, as stated, to glorify His Son.

Point of Truth: The things you do in your body, By DESIRE, is the real you.

Notice some things God says about our desires in the following passage.

Psalm 37:3 **Trust in the Lord, and do good; so shalt thou dwell in the land, and verily thou shalt be fed. 4 Delight thyself also in the Lord: and he shall give thee the desires of thine heart. 5 Commit thy way unto the Lord; trust also in him; and he shall bring it to pass. 6 And he shall bring forth thy righteousness as the light, and thy judgment as the noonday.**

Read this passage very thoughtfully. Sandwiched between two admonishments to **trust** God is the call to **delight** in Him and the promise that He will put His **desires** in your heart. When your **desires** and God's are the same, He **brings** them to **pass** to reveal your righteous heart so it can clearly be seen, which glorifies Jesus by manifesting His power to transform sinners like us into saints. God's will for your life is ALL About JESUS!

When it is in your heart to do God's will before you know what it is, no matter what He might reveal, at that point you are trusting Him and are sacrificially surrendered to Him. God sees when you are so surrendered to Him that you will strive to do His will, whatever it might be. Don't wait to know what He wants before you surrender your all to Him. Sacrificially surrender your all to Him now. Do this based on the love that He continually shows to you, and you will not miss His will.

Point of Truth: The first step in discovering God's will is to be fully surrendered to Him in advance because you know He loves you.

God loves you and is working to make you like His Son, thus, a living manifestation of His grace, which fulfills His Highest Purpose for you.

Being made like Jesus, conformed to His image, includes you standing in truth and victory over yourself and the powers of this world.

In full surrender to Jesus, you are finding your **delight** in Him. When He see your **trust** and **delight** in Him, He will put His **desires** in your heart and they become your desires.

Point of Truth: God's desires and the sacrificially surrendered person's desires always work out to be the same.

Example: When God calls someone to be a missionary in a foreign land where living conditions are tough. The surrendered person comes to desire to be there because he/she desires God and is striving to do His will no matter what it is, no matter the cost.

Discovering God's will is more about focusing your heart and life on Jesus than it is the things He wants to do through and for you.

As strange as it may seem, God uses our desires to direct us in His will. And, when and if our desires are not in line with His will, He uses at least two things to keep us on track.

1. Peace in our hearts, or a lack of peace when a thing we may want or think is His will is not. (See Col.3:15)

2. Opened or Closed doors of opportunity. God opens or closes doors of opportunity to protect and guide us into His will. (See 1 Cor,. 16:9; 2 Cor. 2:12; Col. 4:3; and Acts 16:6-7).

God sees your heart. He knows if you delight in Him. He knows whether you delight and desire to do His will or not.

I am not saying everything we do in the Christian life is done because we always want to do it that way. At times, we don't want to do difficult things. What I am saying is we can want

Jesus so much, to be all His in every way, that we make hard choices to do His will because we love and trust Him.

Point of Truth: We will simply trust God to lead and care for us when we are trusting Him.

That is what trusting Him is. It is trusting Him, especially when we are not sure what to do or when we know what His will is and it is difficult.

Example: When God called me to preach and become a pastor, He gave me a desire to do so. I was not by nature or practice one who thought myself a good choice to lead a church. I was a farmer and planned to be so through my life. But, God changed my desires. He gave me His desires and they became my desires.

I have not always desired to do everything required to be a pastor, but I have continued to desire to do God's will, so I accept, as His will, the favorable and unfavorable things associated with my calling.

So, sacrificially surrender your all to Jesus. With all of your heart, in love-driven passion, go after Jesus and His glory and He will fulfill His will in you.

As you turn your heart toward God, you will more and more see yourself as the glorious miracle that He says you are in His Son.

In this writing I have sought to make everything about Jesus Christ, because as the Bible teaches, everything in God's plan is about Him. Therefore, our lives, when right, are as well.

I don't fear that one day I will stand before God and hear Him say, "You took my Son too seriously. You made too much of Him." But, I do fear many will have been religious, even dedicated to His work (Matthew 7:21-23) without ever realizing Who Jesus is and how important it is to know Him personally, to depend on Him completely and to live a love-driven life in pursuit of Him.

Point of Truth: You can't make too much of Jesus, but you can make far too little of Him.

Week One, Day One
Walking with God and Understanding Your Heart.
God Sees Your Heart.

 Memory verse–Prov. 4:23 **Keep thy heart with all diligence; for out of it are the issues of life.**

All that comes from one's life comes from a source in him/her. The **heart** is that source. God made us with a part which He calls the "**heart**." Some of the things you will study about your heart are:

-It is an unseen part of your life that you control. You choose the focus of your heart;

-You are able to know where your heart is given at all times;

-The heart is God's way of evaluating the intentions of your life;

- God works in a person's life according to the spiritual condition of his/her heart.

-It is a major part of the way you assess your own spiritual condition.

-Where your heart is given, greatly influences your thoughts, desires and decisions.

-Your heart has a huge impact on your words and the intentions by which they are spoken.

The first time the word "**heart**" is mentioned in the Bible is in Genesis 6:5 **And God saw that the wickedness of man was great in the earth, and that every imagination of the thoughts of his <u>heart</u> was only evil continually. 6 And it repented the LORD that he had made man on the earth, and it grieved him at his <u>heart</u>.** This is the record of how God evaluated mankind before He sent the worldwide flood during the time of Noah. Notice verse five: "**God saw . . .**" God saw man's heart and the wicked thoughts and actions coming from it.

The word "**imagination**" means *conception*. The heart is where thoughts are born. Check the memory verse. When God saw man's "**heart was only evil continually**," He destroyed everyone but Noah and his family.

The word "**heart**" in verse five is the same Hebrew word for "**heart**" in verse six. Man was created with a "**heart**" as God has a "**heart**." Your decisions, choices, words, and lifestyle proceed from your heart. Your life is a reflection of your heart. Your heart reveals what you love, and whatever you love compels and drives your life.

Point of Truth: You have a heart just as God has a heart.

The paths you have taken in life have been greatly influenced by your heart. Your words and the way you speak them, as a pattern, are directly connected to your heart. Luke 6:45 **A good man out of the good treasure of his heart bringeth forth that which is good; and an evil man out of the evil treasure of his heart bringeth forth that which is evil: for of the abundance of the <u>heart his mouth speaketh</u>.** There is another insightful thought in this verse. The word "**treasure**" basically means *a place where valuables are stored* or *whatever one estimates as "most valuable;" "most important;" therefore, "most precious."* If a person treasures money, then money will be most important to him/her. Notice how Jesus made a clear connection between what you **treasure** and your **heart** in Matthew 6:21 **For where your treasure is, there will your heart be also.** Whatever you **treasure**, (estimate as most valuable) your heart soon goes there. The more you treasure Jesus, the closer you will walk with Him.

When the prophet Samuel was sent by God to anoint the second king over the nation of Israel, God gave deep insight into His manner of judging each person. (See 1 Samuel 16:1-13). When the prophet saw David's eldest brother, he assumed he was the one to anoint as king, but he wasn't. 1 Samuel. 16:7 **But the LORD said unto Samuel, Look not on his countenance, or on the height of his stature; because I have refused him: for the LORD seeth not as man seeth; for man looketh on the outward appearance, but <u>the LORD looketh on the heart</u>**. Man looks **"on the outward appearance, but the Lord looketh on the heart."** God saw how David's heart was about seeking, loving and knowing Him more deeply. David was a man after God's heart.

You can give your heart to all sorts of things. Your heart can be given in part or in total. You may have given your heart to others, such as the approval of peers, a lover, leaders, gangs, etc. Many have given their hearts to wealth (money, houses, etc.). Others have given their hearts to themselves, which is manifested in pride, arrogance, boasting, and self-promotion. Others have given their hearts to success, such as careers/jobs, education, talents, and gifts. Others have given their hearts to comforts, recreation, and fun. Some have given their hearts to rebellion or other sins, such as immorality, anger, or abuse of drugs or alcohol.

Whatever has your heart has a controlling influence on your life. Many have suffered much because their hearts were given to things that led them to violate God and His Word. No doubt, there are other things to which one's heart may be given.

You may have set your heart on Jesus. If you've kept it there, and have learned to pursue Him in a love-driven relationship, you are living a spiritually fruitful life with confident anticipation of the wonderful future God has for you.

Whatever you live for has your heart, your life. Wherever your heart is, there your life and loyalties are. You desire to be with whatever or whoever has your heart. A person will sacrifice almost everything, if not everything, to have whatever or whoever has his/her heart.

This relationship between God and man has God-given guidelines. One can only come to God in His way. When God calls a person to Himself, He calls him/her to come to Him through His Son, the Lord Jesus Christ. God says in John 14:6 **Jesus saith unto him, I am the way, the truth, and the life: no man cometh unto the Father, but by me.**

When someone does come to God through Jesus, that person must come by believing in Him in his/her heart and confessing Him as the Lord He is. Romans 10:9 **That if thou shalt confess with thy mouth the Lord Jesus, and shalt <u>believe in thine heart</u> that God hath raised him from the dead, thou shalt be saved. 10 For <u>with the heart</u> man believeth unto righteousness; and with the mouth confession is made unto salvation.** The word **"believe"** was commonly used as a banking term in ancient times. It meant to deposit money/valuables for safekeeping. As in our day a person might *"put in trust"* his/her valuables to a bank for safekeeping.

Believing in Jesus is not mere knowledge that He exists. It is trusting in Him to the point of receiving Him as one's own Lord and Savior, thus entrusting one's life and all to Him. And when a person put faith in Jesus, He saves him/her by His own power and grace. John 1:12 **But as many as <u>received</u> him, to them gave he power to become the sons of God,**

> The word "believe" was translated from the Greek word *"pisteuo"--to have faith in . . . to entrust, especially one's spiritual well being to Christ, to put in trust with.-* Strong's Greek Dictionary #4100

even **to them that believe on his name:**

The Bible teaches turning to God (repentance) by faith in Jesus is the way of salvation. Acts 20:21 **Testifying both to the Jews, and also to the Greeks, repentance toward God, and faith toward our Lord Jesus Christ.**

God's plan before the world was created is that His Son, Jesus Christ, be recognized and exalted as the Lord He was, is, and will forever be. Jesus is Lord! And everyone who is surrendered to Him as his/her Lord and Savior, is saved. Luke 24:45 **Then opened he their understanding, that they might understand the scriptures, 46 And said unto them, Thus it is written, and thus it behooved Christ to suffer, and to rise from the dead the third day: 47 And that repentance and remission of sins should be preached in his name among all nations, beginning at Jerusalem.**

1. As honestly as you can, write where your heart is now. _____
2. List in the column some things you gave your heart to in the past.

It is likely that you have given your heart to things other than God, if so, ask Him to forgive you. If you are in bondage to a certain sin, ask God to show you how He wants to make you free. If Jesus is your Lord, He does want you to be completely free from the bondage of sins. Romans 6:14 declares, "**For sin shall not have dominion over you. . . .**" Believe God's Word!

3. If you are not sure that you are saved, or you know you are not, please place your faith in Jesus Christ as your own Lord and Savior. Pray, crying out to Him from your heart in repentance and faith in Him. You might pray the example prayer of repentance and faith in the box.

If you struggle being sure God will accept you in salvation, you must know He accepts us only in His Son and saves us for His Son.

The following passage is given as an analogy of a courtroom. God is on His throne, with Jesus at His right hand. Picture that scene in your mind as you read Romans 8:31 **What shall we then say to these things? If God be for us, who can be against us? 32 He that spared not his own Son, but delivered him up for us all, how shall he not <u>with him</u> also <u>freely</u> give us all things? 33 Who shall lay any thing to the charge of God's elect? It is <u>God that justifieth</u>. 34 Who is he that condemneth? It is <u>Christ that died</u>, yea rather, that is risen again, who is even at the right hand of God, who also maketh intercession for us.**

Do you really think God would give Jesus to die for everyone who believes and trusts in Him and His sacrificial death to pay our sin debts, and then reject we who believe in Him? Jesus died to redeem you unto Himself. What He ask of you is for you to trust Him by relying on Him as your Lord and Savior, so do it, if you have not.

When you know the Judge of the universe gave His Son to pay your sin debt, to settle all that will ever be against you, you can rest assured that He has accepted His payment (His Son) as more than enough. You can know God will not reject Himself. He gave Himself in death on your behalf for His own glory now and forever.

The words **with him** (v. 32) show God gave His Son to save us, and **with Him,** He surely gives us all that is needed to justify us fully and freely. Everyone who receives Jesus, has eternal life and **with him** comes everything needed to fully justify him/her. Make sure, above all things that you have received Jesus Christ as your Lord and Savior.

"Dear God, I am a sinner. Please forgive me.
I believe Jesus died in my place and rose from the dead.
I believe and confess Him as Lord and Savior of my life.
I receive Him as the greatest gift of Your love.
I repent, therefore, I turn from serving sin and myself to serve my Lord Jesus.
Help me learn to walk with Him in love-driven faithfulness, with all of my heart. Amen."

---

1 John 5:12
He that hath the Son hath life; *and* **he that hath not the Son of God hath not life.**

Week One, Day Two
Walking with God and Understanding Your Heart.
God Gives "A New Heart."

 Memory verse– Proverbs 4:23 **Keep thy heart with all diligence; for out of it are the issues of life.**

God told His prophet, Samuel, to anoint a man named "Saul" as Israel's first king. The following passage is an insightful record of that anointing. Through Saul's life, God teaches many things about one's heart. 1 Samuel 9:26 **And they arose early: and it came to pass about the spring of the day, that Samuel called Saul to the top of the house, saying, Up, that I may send thee away. And Saul arose, and they went out both of them, he and Samuel, abroad. 27 And as they were going down to the end of the city, Samuel said to Saul, Bid the servant pass on before us, (and he passed on,) but stand thou still a while, that I may show thee the word of God. 10:1 Then Samuel took a vial of oil, and poured it upon his head, and kissed him, and said, Is it not because the LORD hath anointed thee to be captain over his inheritance? 2 When thou art departed from me to day, then thou shalt find two men by Rachel's sepulchre in the border of Benjamin at Zelzah; and they will say unto thee, The asses which thou wentest to seek are found: and, lo, thy father hath left the care of the asses, and sorroweth for you, saying, What shall I do for my son? 3 Then shalt thou go on forward from thence, and thou shalt come to the plain of Tabor, and there shall meet thee three men going up to God to Bethel, one carrying three kids, and another carrying three loaves of bread, and another carrying a bottle of wine: 4 And they will salute thee, and give thee two loaves of bread; which thou shalt receive of their hands. 5 After that thou shalt come to the hill of God, where is the garrison of the Philistines: and it shall come to pass, when thou art come thither to the city, that thou shalt meet a company of prophets coming down from the high place with a psaltery, and a tabret, and a pipe, and a harp, before them; and they shall prophesy: 6 And the spirit of the LORD will come upon thee, and thou shalt prophesy with them, and shalt be turned into another man. 7 And let it be, when these signs are come unto thee, that thou do as occasion serve thee; for God is with thee. 8 And thou shalt go down before me to Gilgal; and, behold, I will come down unto thee, to offer burnt offerings, and to sacrifice sacrifices of peace offerings: seven days shalt thou tarry, till I come to thee, and show thee what thou shalt do. 9 And it was so, that when he had turned his back to go from Samuel, God gave him another heart: and all those signs came to pass that day.**

Notice how God prepared Saul to be king. 1 Samuel 10:6 "**turned into another man.**" And,"**God gave him another heart:**" (v.9). God didn't give Saul a manual on How to Be King. He gave him "**another heart.**" Samuel told Saul he would know what to do at each "**occasion . . . because God is with thee**" (v.7).

History reveals Saul did not continue to walk closely with God. In fact, after two years of successfully walking with Him, he became rebellious. Saul knew what was right or wrong by the "**heart**" God had given him. King Saul often went against his heart. Therefore, God removed him from being king and did not allow his sons to reign after him.

God replaced Saul and his family with David his descendants. Notice the first prophecy God gave concerning Saul's replacement.

1 Samuel 13:13 **And Samuel said to Saul, Thou hast done foolishly: thou hast not kept the commandment of the LORD thy God, which he commanded thee: for now would the LORD have established thy kingdom upon Israel for ever. 14 But now thy kingdom shall not continue: the LORD hath sought him <u>a man after his own heart</u>, and the LORD hath commanded him to be captain over his people, because thou hast not kept that which the LORD commanded thee.**

Saul did not keep his heart after God, so he didn't continue to do His will, therefore, God "**. . . sought him a man after his own heart . . ..**" A study of 1 Samuel reveals Saul's heart shifted away from God. After which, his life became a pattern of disobedience and rebellion. A careful study shows Saul sought to keep his kingdom more than anything else. His heart shifted to his position as king, rather than, keeping it on God, Who gave him that place of leadership.

Even God-appointed things (blessings) can steal one's heart away from Him. Jesus is not looking for persons merely committed to His work or the other blessings He has entrusted to us. He is looking for persons who are first and foremost surrendered to Him. When Jesus has your heart, you will want to do His will, and He will accomplish His work through you. There is a commitment to His work, but only out of heart-surrender to Him, where all is viewed as belonging to Him. You actually own nothing. You merely manage everything God has entrusted to your care. Even your time (your life span) is in God's hands. It too belongs to Him.

Many are committed to places of service in Christ's work, but their lives and attitudes are unlike Him. This reveals their hearts are not in the process of turning to Him. Thus, they are not walking closely with Him. When your heart is set upon Jesus, the place of service will become less-and-less important. At that point you will not be as concerned with the greatness of a position or place of service, but will desire to know you are in God's will. When your heart is lovingly set upon Jesus, He is treasured above all.

Saul shifted his heart away from God to his position as king. He permitted the deceitful lure of his high position to have his heart. Once his heart shifted, his actions, attitudes and words revealed his heart was not right with God. Be careful with God-given places of honor, success and service. Such blessings can steal your heart away from Him. When your heart shifts away from Jesus to anything, good or bad, you lose the joy that He wants for you. Because true joy is only in Jesus, not the things He entrusts to you.

Has your heart shifted to a blessing God has entrusted to you to mange for Him?

Every way of a man is right in his own eyes: but the LORD pondereth the hearts.
Proverbs 21:2

Week One, Day Three
Walking with God and Understanding Your Heart.
Living and Loving Effectively by Giving All to Jesus.

 Memory verse– Proverbs 4:23 **Keep thy heart with all diligence; for out of it are the issues of life**.

Like King Saul, many are in bondage and confusion because they have given their hearts to their positions rather than keeping them fixed on Jesus. Even places of service in the church can become a personal kingdom in those who fail to keep their hearts turned to Jesus. This is one of the root causes of conflict between members. When their hearts shift away from Jesus to their positions in His church, or the prestige that comes with places of leadership, trouble always follows. At this point their joy becomes connected to those positions, thus very unstable. However, those who keep their hearts on Jesus, find His joy sustaining them, even in times of trouble. They have joy because they know God loves them and with love-driven faith, they trust Him. Therefore, even when they are hurting, there is sustaining trust, peace and joy deep in their souls because they know they are trusting God, Who is faithful to see them through whatever He allows.

It doesn't take a major shift in one's heart to have loss of joy. It can simply be the result of not remaining in close fellowship with Jesus. Walking in love-driven fellowship with Jesus is the most important thing in a believer's life. Jesus said in John 15:7 **If ye abide in me, and my words abide in you, ye shall ask what ye will, and it shall be done unto you. 8 Herein is my Father glorified, that ye bear much fruit; so shall ye be my disciples. 9 As the Father hath loved me, so have I loved you: continue ye in my love. 10 If ye keep my commandments, ye shall abide in my love; even as I have kept my Father's commandments, and abide in his love. 11 These things have I spoken unto you, that my joy might remain in you, and** *that* **your joy might be full.**

There are three things taught in this passage that cause Jesus to flow His **joy** through a person (like a vine flows life through its branches, which is the context of this passage). They are:

1. "**Abiding**" in Jesus through <u>love based</u> fellowship (therefore always believing and knowing God loves you, 1 John 4:16. Knowing God loves you may seem to be a given, but for many it is definitely not. Many need to know and believe God really does love them).

2. His "**words**" abiding in you. This means keeping His words to you fresh in your heart and life.

3. Keeping His "**commandments**" which Jesus equates with loving Him (Also see John 14:21-23). Out of love-driven interaction with Jesus, flows love-driven striving for obedience.

Jesus gave these three in the context of your prayer life (v. 7). As we shall see, your prayer life has a significant part of God fulfilling His Highest Purpose for creating you. An effective prayer life is imperative to stay on track in your love-driven pursuit of Jesus and His will.

Notice verse 8 **Herein is my Father glorified, that ye <u>bear</u> much fruit; so shall ye be my disciples.** The Greek word translated "**bear**" does not mean *to produce*. It means to *carry or to hold up*. The vine produces the fruit. The branches merely *"hold up"* the fruit. Jesus is the vine and each believer is a branch. John 15:5 **I am the vine, ye** *are* **the branches: He that abideth in me,**

and I in him, the same bringeth forth much fruit: for without me ye can do nothing.

The Christian life is ALL about Jesus. When you read verses five through eleven, you see it is Jesus Who produces fruit through His followers (us). As we walk in fellowship with Him, we strive to obey Him in love (vs. 10-11). In His love for us and our love for Him, we "hold up" the fruit He produces through us. When our hearts are right, our love for Jesus drives our obedience (and the world sees the love that motivates us to do good things) and this glorifies our Father. Keeping commandments is to always be about love. To be right, obedience is never about law, duty or obligation, because there is no joy in these, but there is great joy in walking with Jesus in love.

When your heart shifts away from Jesus to anything else, His joy doesn't flow through you as it should. His joy is not circumstantial. It is based on knowing Jesus loves you and will see you though whatever you face because you are striving to abide in Him. A heart shifted away from Jesus will result in not walking closely with Him. Then all of life loses the joy and glow that love-driven fellowship with Him adds to it.

Many husbands are confused because they are seeking to be what God wants, but they know something inside isn't right. Many wives are the same. Christian dads and moms are in the same condition concerning their children. For this same reason many are confused and often in conflict with one another. They are trying, or have tried, to be right with God. They want to be, but they know things are not right in their spiritual lives. They do not understand where the problem lies. They have not considered to what or to whom their hearts are given. They do not realize they have a heart problem.

At times, people give up on ministry, families, and even life because they have tried to be effective and fruitful in life, but have failed. Their failure may not have been in their efforts. Their failure was likely because Jesus did not have their hearts. Therefore, He was not flowing His joy through them as He wanted. They were living their lives, and maybe even trying to do God's work, in the power of their flesh, which always leads to emptiness and frustration.

Your family does not need parents with hearts given to them above God. What they need more than all else is a dad and mom who do right day-by-day because they have hearts that treasure Jesus more than anything. When your heart is right with Him, your love for others is at its best, because it is driven by love for Jesus and His glory. You will not love your family less, but rather more purely in the will and ways of God and your family will see your love for Jesus and that is what impacts their lives for Him.

Point of Truth: You can't love your family too much, but you can show your love for them in misguided ways.

The love you show to your family and others cannot be at its best when you are not walking closely with Jesus. Daily fellowship with Jesus gives place for His love to flow through you. One indication of a heart away from Jesus is a person's love will be controlling and possessive toward others, rather than liberating, fruitful and fulfilling.

Your church family does not need persons with their hearts given to their places of ministry in possessive ways. Because once the heart shifts to a place of ministry, that place becomes a "personal kingdom" in that person. Then, they become controlling and self-serving (just like King Saul did with his God-appointed place of service). Believers must consistently

give our places of service back to Jesus or we risk possessing them for ourselves, while thinking our lives are pure. Many who have possessed a place of service in the church think they are right because they're doing a good work and rightly gain a sense of significance by serving there. They do not realize their hearts are given to that ministry, when it should be given to Jesus. When your ministry becomes more important to you than Jesus, that lets you know your heart has shifted, and needs to return to Him.
If needed:

    a. give your ministries in Jesus' church back to Him.
    b. give your family members, one-by-one, back to Jesus.
    c. give your job or career back to Jesus.
    d. give your possessions back to Jesus.
    e. give your recreation and things you enjoy back to Jesus.
    f. give your struggles, pains and sorrows to Jesus while looking to Him as your source of refuge, help and hope.

One sure way you can tell you have given all persons and things back to Jesus is by the fact that you do not intentionally use them selfishly.

Above all, be sure you are regularly spending time in prayer and fellowship with Jesus in His Word. Do these with your focus on Him, on loving Him, on spending time with Him in love-driven pursuit of Him.

> "The world has yet to see what God can do with a man who is fully and wholly consecrated to Him."
> -Henry Varley, Endnote 10, p. 304.

Whatever you make of Jesus, in loving Him, determines how spiritually fruitful and joyous your life will be.

It is not your religious experiences, reforming or works, that make you righteous in God's sight. Only Jesus can make you righteous before His perfect justice. And He does that totally by His own righteousness, which is imputed to every believer when He saved him/her.

Out of knowing Jesus is your righteousness in salvation, there is a personal striving to live righteously, and that is only acceptable with God when it is focused on His Son, therefore done out of love for Him. (See 1 Corinthians chapter 13).

Jesus is God's Everything and whenever you grasp this truth and go after Him with all of your heart, you then know walking in fellowship, moment-by-moment with Him is the most important thing. Because out of that intimate fellowship, that love-driven relationship, you strive to do His will, thus to be given to Him in every area of your life.

It is true, "**IT IS ALL ABOUT JESUS!** Are you striving for your life to be all about Him? _____

Week One, Day Four
Walking with God and Understanding Your Heart.
A Heart Ready to Turn at Any Point.

 Memory verse– Proverbs 4:23 **Keep thy heart with all diligence; for out of it are the issues of life**.

In this lesson you will read of multiple promises God makes to His surrendered people. He longs to bless us and make our lives joyful, fruitful and fulfilling. Deuteronomy 30:9 **And the LORD thy God will make thee plenteous in every work of thine hand, in the fruit of thy body, and in the fruit of thy cattle, and in the fruit of thy land, for good: for the LORD will again <u>rejoice over thee for good</u>, as he rejoiced over thy fathers: 10 If thou shalt hearken unto the voice of the LORD thy God, to keep his commandments and his statutes which are written in this book of the law,** *and* **if thou <u>turn</u> unto the LORD thy God with all thine <u>heart</u>, and with all thy soul.**

Think of God rejoicing over you. Considered how He rejoices over you when you live in a love-driven passion of Jesus. Imagine, how He smiles over you when He sees you striving to love and honor Jesus with all of your heart. He knows exactly what your humanity is like.

God knows the self-bent corruption that is in everyone of us. He knows the battles we face against this world, our own fleshly desires, and the forces of evil who tempt us, and constantly lie to us. So, when He sees you with your heart after His Son, He rejoices over you.

You are studying about two types of turning your heart to God. I call each "a point of turning."

Example #1: Suppose God convicts someone of sinful anger (as He did me. You will read about this at the end of week two). At that point, one is brought to conviction to clearly recognize and face his/her sin. A person is in rebellion if he/she refuses to turn as fully as he/she can in confession and repentance. The moment a person is made aware of a sin, God expects him/her to make adjustments in life and lifestyle to surrender to Him. So, one way a "point of turning" takes place is when one turns from a certain sin to walk with Jesus in love-driven obedience.

Example #2: Suppose God is calling you to a particular ministry position in the church. You become convinced God would have you surrender and make all adjustments in life to follow by faith. God will bring you to a "point of turning." At that point, you must yield to the Holy Spirit and begin doing that ministry. If you do it, driven by love for Jesus, He will change you as you serve Him there. So, another way a "point of turning" takes place is when you come to understand a calling and surrender to it.

When you are striving to have your heart fixed on Jesus, you are willing to <u>humble</u> yourself and strive to become the person He wants. At this point you are willing to obediently follow Jesus in every way no matter the costs. And, you have given everything to Him and are ready to follow Him by faith wherever He leads and opens the door of opportunity.

I say "turning your heart to God is a process," because it is a daily <u>striving</u> to be given to Him in every way. No one does this perfectly, but many desire and strive to do so.

God looks at our hearts when He examines us. When He finds your heart desiring to be turned to Jesus, thus making adjustments in your life to please

Him because you love Him, He will by grace, change your life. (It is God's grace that causes you to want to do His will. See Phil. 2:13).

When it comes to being effective in life, the intentions of your heart, when right with God, overshadow the reality that you are not perfect. Therefore, it is the "**intents**" of our hearts that make and keep us usable in God's hands. Hebrews 4:12 **For the word of God is quick, and powerful, and sharper than any twoedged sword, piercing even to the dividing asunder of soul and spirit, and of the joints and marrow, and is a <u>discerner of the thoughts and intents of the heart</u>**.

"Humility is simply living in the truth and character of God, and living in personal dependence on God as Creator and Savior."
--Gordon T. Smith, Endnote 9, p. 307.

Week One, Day Five
Walking with God and Understanding Your Heart.
A Man after God's Heart.

 Memory verse– Proverbs 4:23 **Keep thy heart with all diligence; for out of it are the issues of life.**

As the prophet Samuel grew older, the people asked for a king. They did not want Samuel's rebellious sons to reign over them. Therefore, God made Saul the first king in Israel. When King Saul turned his heart away from God, he became disobedient to His clearly defined will. So God sent Samuel to anoint David to take Saul's place. God declared that Saul's replacement would be "**a man after His own heart**." The following passage sheds more light on this. Acts 13:21 **And afterward they desired a king: and God gave unto them Saul the son of Cis, a man of the tribe of Benjamin, by the space of forty years. 22 And when he had removed him, he raised up unto them David to be their king; to whom also he gave testimony, and said, I have found David the son of Jesse, a man after mine own heart, which shall fulfil all my will.**

"**Fulfilling**" God's will is an outflow of a heart that is striving for His heart. What are you after in your relationship with God? Are you after His heart or merely things He can do for you? This makes all of the difference to Him.

What did God say David was? ". . . a _____ after mine own _____ . . ." What does God say a man after His "**own heart**" will do? ". . . which shall _____ all my will." Was David's heart primarily after things from God's hand or God's heart? _____ This is reflected in the prayers and Psalms of David. He sought an intimate relationship with God. He treasured God and intimacy with Him. David learned what God really desires from a person is not sacrifice from an obligation type of approach to Him, but of love and intimacy where a person gladly offers sacrifices to Him for His pleasure. David said, **My soul followeth hard after thee: thy right hand upholdeth me,** Psalm 63:8. You can pursue Jesus like that too, if you will.

Some have asked: "If David did God's will, then what about his sin with Bathsheba, the wife of Uriah?" (David committed adultery with Uriah's wife, then had Uriah killed at war so he could have her as his own wife, 1 Sam. 11-12). 1 Kings 15:5 **Because David did that which was right in the eyes of the LORD, and turned not aside from any thing that he commanded him all the days of his life, save only in the matter of Uriah the Hittite.** God tells how David's heart departed from Him in that matter. David did as one might tragically do. He did not listen to God's convicting voice when tempted, therefore he "**turned . . . aside**" from walking with God. He went against God's known will, breaking His commandments. David was forgiven by God but reaped great consequences from his sins. Every believer is completely forgiven in Christ (and that solely by His redeeming blood).

A real Christian expects to go to Heaven on the virtue of another.
–A. W. Tozer, Endnote 10, p. 196.

No one lives sinlessly. But many live, and have lived, victoriously. As a believer, you can live above the dominion of any particular sin by obediently walking with Jesus by faith with your heart after Him. You should never believe you must remain trapped in bondage (under the controlling power) to a certain sin. When the Holy Spirit sheds light on your sin (points out a certain sin by bringing conviction), God is ready and willing to free you as you turn to Christ in confession and repentance (although, at times, there may be the need to learn how to win over temptation's controlling power, as we will soon study). You will remain free as long as you stay in the process of turning your heart to Jesus, thus, continuing to walk closely with Him in a love-compelled striving for obedience.

Point of Truth: Jesus is God's Answer and Remedy for everything we need and you find His fullness when you abide in His love (See John 15:9).

Make your heart and life about loving Jesus and He will bring you to the place to live victoriously over sin's controlling power!

Some claim to walk in fellowship with God while living in sinful lifestyles. That is impossible. God says in 1 John 1:6 **If we say that we have fellowship with him, and walk in darkness, we lie, and do not the truth: 7 But if we walk in the light, as he is in the light, we have fellowship one with another, and the blood of Jesus Christ his Son cleanseth us from all sin. 8 If we say that we have no sin, we deceive ourselves, and the truth is not in us.** One aspect of God's judgement on those who claim God approves of their sins is He sends darkness, spiritual blindness, upon them. In that spiritual blindness, they really do think God approves of their sins.

To walk in victorious fellowship with God, you must admit your sins and face the fact that they are not acceptable to Him. One sure indication of the need of personal revival is when one realizes his/her sins but doesn't love Jesus enough to repent. The reason a believer can become satisfied to allow a particular sin in his/her life is because there is a lack of living in love-driven fellowship with Jesus, thus something else has his/her heart.

Those who are victorious over sins have gained that victory by focusing on maintaining close fellowship with Jesus above all else. He has become more important to them than anything, especially their sinful desires. Victorious Christians continue to be tempted and occasionally stumble, but they do not intend to commit deliberate acts of sin. They are not perfect, but they are victorious as they choose to have their hearts turning to Jesus moment-by-moment. They are given victory because of their faith in Him. Their intentions are to please Him in every way, because they know with all certainty that He loves them, because He says He does, and His Word is true.

Many believers do not struggle with the fact that Jesus alone did all that was needed for our salvation. But many of those same believers do not trust Him concerning overcoming particular, habitual sins. The power to save you is Jesus' power and the power to conquer each sin is His too. Desiring Jesus and His approval drives devoted believers in all we do. God knows what you truly desire. If you desire Jesus for who He is, He will work in you to bring you into the victory He has gained for us. This is part of the Biblical process called "sanctification." God has promised to complete the work He began in you. Philippians 1:6 **Being confident of this very thing, that he which hath begun a good work in you will perform it until the day of Jesus Christ:**

1. Is there an area in your life where you know you need to turn your heart to God? _____

2. Can you identify an area/s of sin where you seem to be trapped, even though you have tried to be free? _____ If so, ask God to forgive you concerning that sin and to show you how to enter into freedom over your sins (which we will study next week).

3. Ask God to clearly teach His truth to you of how He desires for you to be free in Jesus and remain free from sin's dominating power.

4. Can you identify a failure, a temptation, where you've tried to please God, to be the person He desires, but you return to that sin over and over? _____ If so, confess it to God by agreeing with Him that it is wrong and must be stopped.

5. Have you settled in your heart that you know and believe God really does love you unconditionally and He wants you for His Son in a love-driven, joyous relationship, so you can display His life-transforming love, grace and glory? _____

You may feel your whole Christian life has been an effort of your own, having lived without your heart seeking to be fixed on Jesus. You may be able to remember times of revival when you did turn to Him as best as you could, thus, you knew you were walking closely with Him. But, not knowing to **"keep your heart with all diligence"** you departed from Him. Then confusion and bondage returned because in some area of your life you didn't keep your heart on Him. You didn't intend to depart. You really didn't know what you had done. Of course, you knew about the sins in your life, but you didn't understand how to keep your heart fixed on Jesus moment-by-moment. Aren't you glad God is merciful? He is working in you now, bringing you to the understanding of a heart that is driven by love for Him. Give Him praise for His great mercy and grace.

Oh let the wickedness of the wicked come to an end; but establish the just: for the righteous God trieth the hearts and reins.
Psalm 7:9

Read the following account of God helping me turn to Him.

CHURCH MINISTRY AND A BIG STEP IN MY JOURNEY TO FREEDOM

I have been on this journey to spiritual freedom since I received Jesus Christ as my Lord and Savior. From that day, He has been working in me to conform me to His image.

In 1983 on a Wednesday night during a church business meeting where I was pastor, things got out of hand and some people became very angry. I was devastated. I tried to stop the arguments, but only became more involved in the conflict. I started to weep while standing before the church. One man (a recent new member) was so offended that he left saying he would not return. Oh No! My life was coming apart at the seams.

Things finally settled down enough to dismiss the service, or verbal wrestling match, or what I now realize was, "another round of a power struggle in that church." I went home hurting very badly. As I lay in bed that night, all I could do was replay in my mind the painful events of that evening. Over and over I tried to discover what I had done wrong during that meeting. I asked myself, "How could I have done a better job of 'running the church?" I thought, "What if I had said this or that." I was confused.

As I sought God, I became more broken. That night I realized what I was experiencing was not the reaction the Bible teaches I was to have. My stomach was tense and knotted. I said to the Lord, "I know you did not call me to this type of life. This does not agree with your Word. I do not have your peace guarding my heart." Phil. 4:7 **And the peace of God, which passeth all understanding, shall keep your hearts and minds through Christ**

Jesus. And Isaiah 26:3 **Thou wilt keep him in perfect peace, whose mind is stayed on thee: because he trusteth in thee.**

I wasn't in any form of peace. I was falling apart on the inside and out. These feelings were not new to me. I was often in that condition but not to that degree because the church problems had not been to that degree.

I told God how I must have made a mistake about His call on my life to be a pastor. I determined I surely was out of His will. I said, "That's it; I'll resign this coming Sunday and start over with my life." But no peace came with such thoughts.

To add to the pressure, our preschool daughter had asked her mom, after seeing me cry, "If preachers had to always stay at the same church?" I realized what was taking place in the heart of our daughter was what I had seen in some other pastors' and church leaders' children. She was developing bitterness and resentment toward the church and its leadership.

When I told my wife "I'm going to quit, because what happened had gone too far and I can't take it any more." She said something like this, (and I should know, I had heard her say it before) "Oh, Larry, you would be miserable if you did not pastor a church. You couldn't stand it." She was right. I couldn't stand being a pastor; it was killing me and I couldn't stand not being a pastor, because I knew that was God's calling. What was I to do?

That night my journey to gaining freedom took another step. Lying there seeking God, I said, "God, I just can't be a pastor. I'm not good at this. You didn't call me to this type of existence and I know that." God has not spoken aloud to me, but He has spoken clearly to my heart. At that moment I realized I wasn't called to carry the burden of things that are out of my control. His Word does not tell me to control the actions of people. He had not told me to make a church successful by my power. He had called me to preach His Word in love, to minister to people, and tell the lost about Jesus. (I did not know until 14 years later that He had not called me to preaching and ministry nearly to the degree that He had called me to Himself).

I determined if God's people did not obey Him, that was His business more than mine. If they did not come to church, they were His people and He could tend to them. I was to work hard in exhorting and encouraging them to be faithful to Him and help them as much as I can, but I cannot force His will on them, nor force my will on them. I started going over the things I was called to do as a Christian and the other things I was called to do as a pastor.

> It is when a crisis arises, that we instantly reveal upon whom we rely.
> - Oswald Chambers (Endnote #15, Aug. 12).

I realized how **the church belongs only to Jesus.** The church is His bride. If she doesn't act right, that is His problem and not my responsibility. I told Him these things. I said, "Lord, I confess I have tried to be the lord of your church. I have tried to carry the weight of sinful men. I have tried to stand in your place. I have thought myself responsible to produce fruit through your people." Then I said, speaking to my knotted, upset stomach, "Stomach you must relax; this is Jesus' church, it is safe with Him." My words cannot express the peace that flooded my life at that moment. I was suddenly at peace. I told God I was ready to serve Him as a pastor until He told me to do something else.

At that point, I did not know exactly what had taken place in me. It was years later when I began learning about the heart that I looked back and saw what took place that night. What I did was turn my heart away from church ministry and back to the God of the church, where He wanted my heart to be. I had given "my" ministry and His church, back to Him. That is why I had an unexplainable peace. He does not want me to give my heart to His things, not even His people or ministries. He wants to have my heart for Himself. Without my heart lovingly set on Jesus, my focus in ministry will <u>not be about Him as it should</u> be, therefore, He will not produce the fruit and get the glory He wants through me.

Point of Truth: Jesus will not give you His peace until your heart is lovingly fixed on Him.

Why would He, when His purpose is for everything to be about Him and His glory?

You can't work hard enough to gain His peace. You can't buy it with commitment to His work. It's not for sale. Your devotion to His church can't produce it. Have you understood the peace you are searching for can only be found in a personal, intimate relationship with Jesus Christ?

Point of Truth: You can trust the church to Jesus and you can trust your life to Him as well. You can trust Jesus with your family, job, troubles and everything else that might be overwhelming you, if you will.

A very liberating truth I am learning concerning life and ministry is a believer really can trust Jesus with the things he/she cannot control. Sinful anger, frustration, and self-pity are visible signs of failing to trust Jesus with things you can't change.

Point of Truth: There is a lot of difference between someone getting angry at a particular time and someone who lives in a state of anger.

A lifestyle of anger, frustration, or self-pity is a visible sign of the fleshly life (the selfish, self-centered life). We who are "holy men" call our anger "frustration;" it doesn't sound as sinful. Actually, it sounds noble. I might have said: "I am frustrated because the work of God is suffering so." Doesn't that sound holy? Shouldn't I be angry over the suffering condition of the church? <u>No</u>. I should be broken and contrite over it, broken in a way of humbly seeking the heart of God, but not angry toward myself or others, even if they have done me wrong. I should humbly cry out to God for revival, seeking His face, turning from all sin as best as I can, but not living in a world of sinful anger and resentment.

If I really have a heart for Jesus, I should abandon everything that is not of Him. I should make the hard choices of repentance and obedience so I can walk in fellowship with Him based on desire for Him.

Many church leaders think they are serving Christ, but actually and unintentionally their work in the church is self-serving. My life was a clear indication of that, and I didn't know it. Most anger is not a righteous indignation, but rather, frustration because of lack of desired results or unfulfilled expectations or because of trying to maintain significance through a place of control. When a person's heart is toward Jesus, the lack of desired results (fruitfulness) will produce brokenness, not anger. Conflict with others in the church over nonessential issues is a sure sign of someone having personally possessed something that belongs to God.

In the past years as a pastor, I refused many times to try to change things which belong to God. I refuse to try to change things that only He can change. I cannot fully express the freedom I now have in life and ministry.

I want you to know, often I tell the Lord about a problem I recognize is His problem. I strive to maintain a pattern of lifting His church and my life to Him in prayer. I tell Him I am willing to be used in any way He chooses to use me as He works out His problems. Often He does use me. I do basically the same things I might have done before. And when my heart is right, my dependence is solely on Him. Dependence on Jesus gives freedom from sin and selfishness. And, He puts His peace in my heart, which is the greatest liberty, because He is that peace. When He changes me, He simply applies who He is to me. Have Him more freshly in my life, being changed into His likeness, lasts longer than the things He gives me to meet my needs.

There are times when I realize I have crossed the line from my part to His part. When I do, I give His church, my life and ministry back to Him. Through the level of tension in my stomach and nerves, I can clearly evaluate whether I am serving by faith or works, by His Spirit or my flesh. His peace lets me know I am walking closely with Him in love-driven faith.

When God's people take possession of His church or ministries (or their own lives) they fight over selfish things and many times do not realize it. And all the while the enemy of God stands off and laughs while we take stomach and nerve medications.

Point of Truth: A person will fight for whatever has his/her heart, even if it means destroying his/her life, family, and even Christ's church.

When your heart shifts away from Jesus, your life becomes self-serving. Self-serving persons damage and destroy individuals and churches without shame and call it serving God and defending what they think is right. This is exactly what King Saul did after his heart turned away from God. When his heart shifted away from God, he became self-focused and that led to severe problems in every part of His life, his kindship and family.

Church leaders often violate clearly written commands in Scripture over their opinions and things they want. Such as, Philippians 2:3 *Let* **nothing** *be done* **through strife or vainglory; but in lowliness of mind let each esteem others better than themselves. 4 Look not every man on his own things, but every man also on the things of others.** If we are truly concerned with things being done "God's way" then why aren't we just as concerned with everything in God's Word, like the verses above and dozens more like them? Why aren't we just as upset about the lack of prayer, evangelism and missions? Could it be because our hearts are not nearly as much about Jesus as ourselves?

Those who are truly contending for the faith live and act like persons of the faith; because more than anything, they don't want to hurt Jesus, because to them, He is EVERYTHING. There are many who mean well, but their hearts have shifted and they don't realize it. They know something is wrong inside themselves, but are unsure what it is. So, very often they blame their lack of peace on someone else.

King Saul blamed his lack of peace on David. Are you serving in your life like King Saul or King David? Saul lived to protect his kingdom and the things he thought gave his life significance. Saul would attempt to destroy anyone who threatened his rule. If you try to take away a "Saul's" control, you will be bitterly attacked. If you are like David, you will not turn on the ones who seek to remove or hurt you, but rather, you will seek God to see what He says and you will be humble before Him and others. Who are you

most like in your life: King Saul or King David? Circle one. When you speak at a church meeting, or to friends about church issues, do you typically speak humbly for Jesus, caring for Him and His causes, or for your own will? ___
_____ An honest examination of your life- (words, attitude and actions), help you determine where your heart is given.

Recently our church family was discussing new carpet for the sanctuary. There was some tension rising over the color to be chosen. I said "no church has ever split over the color of the carpet." Immediately, some responded with knowledge of a church that did. I responded, "They did not split over the color of the carpet, but rather, they split over who was going to decide the color of the carpet." I can tell you with confidence that Jesus doesn't care which color is chosen, but He does care about each one's actions, attitudes and words as we interact with one another in the process. The color chosen will not matter in eternity, but how Jesus and others are considered and treated by each will.

When I face adversity, I try to remember to tell myself the following to remind me to run to the heart of Jesus as my only place of refuge: **This is a test. It is only a test. Had this been an actual work of God to destroy me, I would not be here. I must tune into God's Word seeking Him with all of my heart for the only reliable information.**

"The nature and depth of pride are illuminated by comparing boasting to self-pity. Both are manifestations of pride. Boasting is the response of pride to success. Self-pity is the response of pride to suffering. Boasting says, "I deserve admiration because I have achieved so much." Self-pity says, "I deserve admiration because I have suffered so much." Boasting is the voice of pride in the heart of the strong. Self-pity is the voice of pride in the heart of the weak. Boasting sounds self-sufficient. Self-pity sounds self-sacrificing.

The reason self-pity does not look like pride is that it appears to be so needy. But the need arises from a wounded ego. It doesn't come from a sense of unworthiness, but from a sense of unrecognized worthiness. It is the response of unapplauded pride.
John Piper, Endnote 12, p. 250

"If you want to know what people are really like, find out what makes them angry, what makes them weep, and what makes them laugh."
--Warren W. Wiersbe, Endnote 11.

Week Two, Day One
Gaining Freedom over Temptation and Sin's Power.
God and His Word are in Your Heart.

 Memory verse– Proverbs 17:3 **The fining pot is for silver, and the furnace for gold: but the LORD trieth the hearts.**

When God saves a person, He gives him/her a new heart. The moment a person is saved, there is something (someone) new in the person that has never been there before. Jesus taught this in John 14:20 **At that day ye shall know that I am in my Father, and ye in me, and I in you.** This was a difficult saying for the disciples to understand. It is a mystery, yet a wonderful reality. We who are saved are in Christ, and He is in us. We are members of His body. You are a member of His body. How do you think He feels about His body, which He gave His life to redeem? _____
What do you think His body will look like when He finishes His work in us?

_____

The following passage helps us better understand how our hearts are involved in gaining freedom over the bondages of sins. 2 Corinthians 3:1 **Do we begin again to commend ourselves? or need we, as some others, epistles** (letters) **of commendation to you, or letters of commendation from you? 2 Ye are our epistle written in our hearts, known and read of all men: 3 Forasmuch as ye are manifestly declared to be the epistle of Christ ministered by us, written not with ink, but with the Spirit of the living God; not in tables of stone, but in fleshly tables of the heart. 4 And such trust have we through Christ to God-ward: 5 Not that we are sufficient of ourselves to think any thing as of ourselves; but our sufficiency is of God; 6 Who also hath made us able ministers of the new testament; not of the letter, but of the spirit: for the letter** (written law) **killeth, but the spirit** (Holy Spirit) **giveth life. 7 But if the ministration of death, written and engraven in stones, was glorious, so that the children of Israel could not stedfastly behold the face of Moses for the glory of his countenance; which glory was to be done away: 8 How shall not the ministration of the spirit be rather glorious? 9 For if the ministration of condemnation be glory, much more doth the ministration of righteousness exceed in glory. 10 For even that which was made glorious had no glory in this respect, by reason of the glory that excelleth. 11 For if that which is done away was glorious, much more that which remaineth is glorious. 12 Seeing then that we have such hope, we use great plainness of speech: 13 And not as Moses, which put a veil over his face, that the children of Israel could not stedfastly look to the end of that which is abolished: 14 But their minds were blinded: for until this day remaineth the same veil untaken away in the reading of the old testament; which veil is done away in Christ. 15 But even unto this day, when Moses is read, the veil is upon their heart. 16 Nevertheless when it shall turn to the Lord, the veil shall be taken away. 17 Now the Lord is that Spirit: and where the Spirit of the Lord is, there is liberty. 18 But we all, with open face beholding as in a glass** (mirror) **the glory of the Lord, are changed into the same image** (Jesus' image) **from glory to glory, even as by the Spirit of the Lord.**

Throughout this chapter God compares the giving of the Ten Commandments to the Holy Spirit given to dwell in the heart of each believer. Notice verse three. The Ten Commandments were given to Moses "**in tables of stone.**" But, now the same commandments are written "**in fleshly tables of the heart**" of believers. Please, do not misunderstand; everyone needs God's written Word to live properly before Him. The heart, apart from God's divine direction, is "**deceitful**" and "**desperately wicked**" (Jer.17:9).

God's righteous standards haven't changed. God knew man could never keep His commandments. They were given to reveal sins and to show how unable we are to live up to His righteous requirements. They were given to help us see how badly we need a Savior to save us. 2 Cor. 3:6 "**for the letter killeth, but the spirit giveth life.**" The "**letter**" that kills is God's Law. Without laws no one feels guilty, because there are no defining points of right and wrong. But, when God's Law came, the people could see how sinful they were by comparing their lives to His Law. Only then could they see how sin justly brings death.

Verses 7-11 tell how "**glorious**" the Ten Commandments were and how they were effective in "**condemnation**" -(forcing God's people to see how they had violated God's law and were deserving of condemnation). God says, "**How shall not the ministration of the spirit be rather glorious?**" If the first standard (God's Law) given to man on stone tablets was "**glorious**," even though it even was effective in condemning people, shouldn't we expect God's Spirit, who is in the heart of every believer giving life and freedom to them, to be much more "**glorious**"? Read verse eleven.

Verses 13-16 tell how people who do not know Christ have a veil over their hearts because their hearts have not turned to Him. In the same way, the believer has a veil over his/her understanding when his/her heart is not turned to Jesus in a particular area.

When your heart is not turned to Jesus based, you don't walk in fellowship with Him, therefore, you do not continue to grow in His likeness. You may improve in keeping rules and Christian things but you are not being changed. You may discipline yourself to more commitment, but the joy of Jesus is not in your daily experience. Being changed is different than merely being better. God is after change in us, which always makes us better.

He has designed our lives to function in a love-driven walk with Jesus, in which we are being transformed into His likeness. Any other reason than love for striving to live an effective Christian life will not succeed. Many serve out of obligation, duty and other man-focused, man-purposed, reasons. But those who have Jesus' joy, have it because they love Him and know He loves them, therefore <u>for Him</u> they strive to please Him. They don't serve a set of rules, they serve Him and this drives them to strive to be the best they can be.

Point of Truth: The Christian Life doesn't work effectively in any other way than through a heart after Jesus, thus a love-driven pursuit of Him.

Notice the word "**it**" of verse sixteen refers to the word "**heart**" of verse fifteen. So the verse could be read: *"Nevertheless, when the heart shall turn to the Lord, the veil shall be taken away."* Your **heart** includes your love, affections and desires.

Then, 2 Cor. 3:17 **Now the Lord is that Spirit: and where the Spirit of the Lord is, there is <u>liberty</u>**. So, we see where the heart turns to Jesus, the Spirit of the Lord gives "moral freedom."

The word "**liberty**" (v. 17) was translated from the Greek word "eleutheria"--freedom (legitimate or licentious, chiefly moral or ceremonial) Strong's #1657

Some might ask, "Aren't those verses in 2 Cor. 3 also referring to those in the Jewish religion?" Yes, but verse 18 reveals how God is making application to His children when He says, "**But we all . . .**" That is why God gave this chapter, to make application to us. He wasn't merely teaching about Old Testament things. He is speaking to us about how He changes us.

When a believer's heart (affections, loves and desires) turns to the Lord he/she is "**changed into the same image from glory to glory, even by the Spirit of the Lord**" (v. 18). The word "**changed**" was translated from the Greek word metamorphoo, (English: metamorphose).

When your heart turns to the Lord, He makes metamorphic changes in you. The more you turn to Jesus in your heart, the more you are changed into His likeness. We are the body of Christ and we are being made like Him by His Spirit.

Point of Truth: When people are taught to live by God's commandments, without first turning their hearts to Him (thus, by a love-driven pursuit of Him), they become mere images of their human teachers, not images of Christ.

Isaiah 29:12 **And the book is delivered to him that is not learned, saying, Read this, I pray thee: and he saith, I am not learned. 13 Wherefore the Lord said, Forasmuch as this people draw near me with their mouth, and with their lips do honour me, but have removed their heart** (affections, care and love) **far from me, and their fear toward me is taught by the precept of men:**

Notice in verse 13, the "**heart**" is "**far**" from God and the result is only a "**taught** obedience" instead of a "relational, love-compelled obedience." Our hearts must first turn to Jesus or we will only be mere images of our human teachers.

When believers live by a taught obedience alone (not focusing on a heart-to-heart relationship with Jesus) they walk in traditions of men instead of God's Spirit. Such believers govern their lives from traditions and rules just as the religious leaders did in Jesus' day.

This is one reason people and churches often have conflict. When people do not have hearts toward Jesus, they don't care about Him and His purposes, so they tend to lean on traditions to get their own selfish wills done. They stand so strongly on their traditions that they do not consider Jesus and His commands to love and always consider one another. Many problems in churches, and families, have to do with selfishness, which many times is expressed in regard to traditions.

When problems arise, and they do, they should drive us to our knees seeking to walk closely with Jesus to discover our part in the trouble (if we caused it) or to get direction. What many need to do is descend from the selfish thrones they have erected inside His church. This is not an uncommon problem. It is doing irreparable damage to individuals, churches, families and communities. I don't want to stand before Jesus someday after having possessed His church or a part of it as my own. And I don't want you to do so either.

In 2 Cor. 3:18, the phrase "**glory to glory**" could be translated "an ongoing, increasing glory" or "step-by-step of glory." As your heart turns to the Lord, the Spirit of God gives liberty/freedom because He is changing you into the moral likeness of Jesus. Freedom and change come by the Holy Spirit's work in us as we turn our hearts more and more to Jesus. Being conformed to His likeness, practically means to think and to act in stride with Him and His Word. Thus, you live in the love of the God the Father, function in Truth that is God the Son, and are being changed by the power of God the Holy Spirit.

God has given His Word to you and written it in your heart. You simply need to focus on keeping "**your heart with all diligence**" in love-driven pursuit of Jesus. As a believer who is seeking to walk closely in fellowship with Jesus, His Word is all you need in order to know the truth. You must consistently take His Word into your heart relationally, on a platform of His love for you and your love for Him, as though it is a love letter written personally to you. I like this definition of truth: "What God says in His Word."

1. Who makes us free when we turn our hearts to Jesus? _____
2. Can The Holy Spirit make you free, and make you more-and-more like Jesus? _____
3. List, in the margin, some ways you are showing you have turned your heart to Jesus, therefore, you are loving and treasuring Him more. Don't be discouraged if you struggle with knowing how and why you should treasure Him more. Coming lessons will show how and why we should.
4. If you struggle with not having a desire to fully turn to Jesus, or the assurance that He will receive you and make you free from the bondage of your sins, ask Him to teach you His truth as you continue through this study.
5. Have you allowed the wrongs of others toward you to cause you to live in bitterness and defeat? _____ If so, confess and ask God to forgive you and to free you as you seek Him.
6. Or, have you allowed hurts from past conflicts to cause you to withdraw from full surrender and devotion to Jesus and His will for you in church ministry to Him and others? _____ If so, place your focus on Jesus and determine to return to serving Him in love with all of your heart.
8. Write the memory verse for this week: _____
_____
_____

Week Two, Day Two
Gaining Freedom over Temptation and Sin's Power.
A Call to Full Surrender.

 Memory verse– Proverbs 17:3 **The fining pot is for silver, and the furnace for gold: but the LORD trieth the hearts.**

It is imperative to realize how your heart is being evaluated by God at all times. He works in and through us according to the spiritual condition of our hearts.

When your heart is turned to Jesus, the Holy Spirit brings you to freedom from bondage of sins step-by-step. If you know you have turned your heart to God and He has <u>not</u> made you free, there must be a "**stronghold**" in your life (your mind), an area where sin has a foothold. 2 Corinthians 10:3 **For though we walk in the flesh, we do not war after the flesh: 4 (For the weapons of our warfare are not carnal, but mighty through God <u>to the pulling down of strong holds</u>;) 5 Casting down <u>imaginations</u>, and every high thing that exalteth itself against the <u>knowledge</u> of God, and bringing into captivity every <u>thought</u> to the obedience of Christ;** A "**stronghold**" is normally erected in a person's mind when he/she practices a sin repeatedly. Verse five speaks of three aspects of the mind: "**imaginations**; **knowledge**; and **thoughts**." You win against sins by knowing and accepting the fact that Jesus really does love you and out of His love for you, you strive to make Him your everything. To do this you must bring **into captivity every thought to the obedience of Christ.** Don't' allow unchristlike thoughts to have a place of residence in your mind. Reject them immediately each time you discover they are trying to have a place in you. Reject them because you know you are striving to love Jesus more than yourself and everything else. Your love for Jesus increases to the degree that you respond in love to His love.

To succumb to temptation and do the sin, you must first lose the battle in your mind. If you think winning is up to you, by your strength, you will not win consistently.

When a sin has become habitual, you can be sure there is a stronghold in your mind. From that stronghold, the forces of sin (the world, your flesh and the devil) fight against the correct way of thinking. When you sin, a **place** is given to the devil. Ephesians 4:27 **Neither give <u>place</u> to the devil.** The word "**place**" could be defined as *an area of jurisdiction*. One can give sin- "**the devil**" a "**place**" in his/her life by sinning, because practicing sins damage proper, Biblical thinking.

The word "**place**" was translated from the Greek word "topos" meaning a *spot* (generally in *space*, but limited by occupancy; . . .) -Strong's # G5117

The places of your mind (where wrong, stinking thinking has a place) that have been surrendered to sin's control must be taken back by turning to Jesus in repentance and confession. You replace the desire for sinning with a more powerful desire for loving Jesus. You willfully practice sins where you think you need to, but you don't need those sins to live the best life, because sin destroys life and joy in everyone it can control. Romans 12:1 **I beseech you therefore, brethren, by the mercies of God, that ye present your bodies a living sacrifice, holy, acceptable unto God, which is your reasonable service. 2 And be not conformed to this world: but be ye transformed by the <u>renewing of your mind</u>, that ye may prove what is that good, and**

acceptable, and perfect, will of God.

Strongholds must be dismantled by God through His truth. To win, you must put truth, God's Word, in the place of the false way of thinking that has a **place** in your mind. **Renewing of your mind** happens as truth is accepted and sacrificially obeyed because you love Jesus and want to please Him.

The **good, and acceptable, and perfect, will of God** is communicated to you when you lovingly focus on Jesus as you study and receive His Word into our mind and heart. At least two things take place as strongholds are destroyed: 1) You learn and accept God's truth. 2) You reject the false thinking, the lies you have believed.

> "The soul can do nothing without the Word of God, and the soul can manage without anything except the Word of God." -Martin Luther

Don't be surprised when you are called to accept and obey truth where your obedience involves sacrifice. Every love-relationship involves sacrificial costs, yet every cost is worth it to have pure, healthy and passionate love.

As a part of Jesus' family you are responsible to feed upon His Word in order to grow in truth and righteous living. As you feed on Jesus' Word with your heart focused on Him, the Holy Spirit transforms your life. "The moment one is born again, he/she is placed into Christ at the highest possible level. A person in Christ cannot gain any more of Him, nor be placed in Him at a higher level. Jesus Christ is received into one's heart in His fullness, but at the same moment the new believer has fully received Christ, he/she is at a low level concerning practical holiness. A new believer is a spiritual baby in Christ. Each new believer must be conformed to His image by the transforming work of the Holy Spirit."[1]

The word "**transformed**" (Rm. 12:2), was translated from the Greek word "metamorphoo" (English-metamorphose, Strong's Gk Dictionary. #G3339).

Each believer must go through stages of metamorphic change as he/she grows in Christ. As your heart turns to Christ out of your growing love-relationship with Him, your mind is renewed to the right way of thinking. Your mind is not renewed until your thinking, what you believe, is aligned with God's Word in such a way that you obey the things He wants because you want to please Him because of Who He is to you, rather than, trying to keep a rule or law.

When God convicts you of His will, He increases the light of your understanding, so you can clearly comprehend it. "The appeal in the opening verse of Romans 12 is for a full surrender, the surrender of the mind, will and emotions to God at a given moment rather than gradually, though the second verse urges the continual yielding of the personality day by day. The degree of yieldedness is governed by the degree of light, and the believer is expected to surrender his life to God as much as he has light on the subject. Further light means further surrender, but a believer cannot surrender more than his all at any given time. . . ."[2]

Some young believers have given all to Jesus, although it may not look that way outwardly. They have surrendered to Him all they know of themselves to all they know of Him and His will at that point. As they grow, God will bring them to "points of turning," thus, to practical, life-style points of surrender. As each one is brought to see issues that need changed in them, they will either follow by faith or they will choose to stay as they are. If they don't learn to relate to Jesus in a love-driven relationship, they are likely to try to do God's will for lesser reasons, such as duty, obligation and such, which lead to loss of joy and discouragement. However if they do follow, striving in love-driven obedience, Jesus keeps His joy flowing in them. If they refuse to love Him enough to follow Him by faith, they lose His joy. God brings us to places to choose to love Jesus enough to make our lives all about Him. With God, everything is always about love and His Son.

Point of Truth: Love drives God is all He does and He is bringing us to the place where love drives us. He is making us to reflect Himself, His glory.

As you remain in a love-driven desire for Jesus and His will, you are showing you are presenting yourself as a "**living sacrifice**" to Him, thus, obeying Romans 12:1. I hope it is in your heart to love Jesus as He wants, and this, because you know He created you so He could have you for Himself.

Any sin (bondage) that has control over your mind, your life, can be removed if you will turn your heart to Jesus, which means to love and treasure Him more than anything as you take proper actions to remove strongholds.

Follow the steps listed below to give place for God to tear down each stronghold. They are steps of repentance and confession. There is nothing special about the wording of these steps of action. They are not a formula. They are simply some practical ways to get to the heart of repentance and confession.

Work through the following five steps very clearly and slowly:

#1. Confess your sins to God (especially where you are in bondage to a sin. Be specific by calling that sin by name). 1 John 1:9 **If we confess our sins, he is faithful and just to forgive us *our* sins, and to cleanse us from all unrighteousness.** The English word "**confess**" comes from two Greek words, "homo" and "logos." Homo means *same* and logos means *word*. So the literal definition of "**confess**" is "to say the *same word* as God says." It means to agree with God and state your agreement. God says sin is wrong, so you must agree. God says sin must be stopped, so stop allowing sin to reign in your life. God says Jesus is the power and authority to forgive and cleanse our lives, thus transform us, so agree with God. Whatever God says, you must agree and confess or your confession is not Biblical confession.

God promises two things to we who "**confess**" our sins. He forgives and cleanses us. Forgiveness deals with our offenses between God and us, thus the guilt and debt we owe. Cleansing deals with removing the stains, dirtiness and dark power of sin's controlling influence. So,

#1. Confess your sins to God.
#2. Claim the cleansing blood of Jesus. (Know that He died to redeem you to Himself and He wants you to be free from sin's control so you can walk in love-driven fellowship with Him, by which He displays His life transforming power in and through you).
#3. Ask God to take back any area where sin has a stronghold in your mind and to tear down that stronghold by renewing your mind. A stronghold only exist because of incorrect thinking. That is what makes it a stronghold. Once your thinking is right, Jesus makes you free (see Jn 8:32).
#4. Devote and surrender that area to Jesus asking Him to reign over your mind (your thoughts you think about yourself and Him) and life.
#5. Praise God for loving you and wanting to change you and make you

free so you can love and exalt His Son.[3]

If you have allowed sin to have a place in you for a long time, do not become discouraged if you do not feel immediate change. One cannot trust one's feelings. True repentance and confession always please God and bring cleansing. A problem can be the mind and heart do not turn easily because a person wants what he/she wants. It takes time spent in close fellowship with Jesus to develop and mature your love for Him. As you spend time with Jesus, focusing on Him as you feed on His Word, your heart will turn more and more to Him. As it does, He will make you free by the Truth He intimately and personally becomes to you.

You will be made free as you turn your heart to Jesus, by which you are transformed step-by-step into His likeness and by being transformed, your mind is renewed. Truthful thinking always wins over false thinking, because truth has the power of God in it, because He is Truth.

As you treasure Jesus more by refusing to practice that sin because your desires are toward Him, He will not fail you.

I cannot stress the importance of practicing steps of cleansing like those above each time you are tempted and seemingly being overpowered. I assure if you will diligently practice these principles, while filling your mind with God's Word as you strive to love Him more deeply, He will break the bondages in your life.

Point of Truth: Your freedom is directly connected to the depth of love you develop for Jesus.

God is All about you loving His Son, thus finding your all in Him.

Luke 24:47 And that repentance and remission of sins should be preached in his (Jesus') **name among all nations, beginning at Jerusalem.**

Thayer Greek Dict. #G3341 Repent

"1) a change of mind, as it appears to one who repents, of a purpose he has formed or of something he has done."

The Greek word for "**repentance**" literally means *a change of mind*. The change is from incorrect thinking to correct thinking. Each time false thinking is rejected and correct thinking becomes a part of your life (to the point that love for Jesus drives your desire to obey Him) you have Biblically repented. Where genuine repentance takes place, your life changes because your heart is turned to Jesus, thus your life is being transformed and your mind renewed.

The reasons I recommend the steps above has a lot to do with the fact that too often "confession" of sins does not focus on any particular act of sin. It is easy to confess sins broadly, thus, not specifically. It is much easier to say, "Lord forgive me of my sins" than "Lord forgive me for _____" (a specific sin). Example: It is better to say, "Forgive me for "being selfish" today when I put myself before others because you say that is wrong. Or, when I "slandered" John Doe. Naming sins makes you more responsible to no longer continue doing them.

Whenever you are tempted to do a specific sin, run to Jesus in your mind and work through the steps above confessing that sin by name.

There are two things taught in the Bible that bring cleansing to one's life. They are the Bible itself (John 15:3) and confession of sins (1 John 1:9). Both of these are based fully on Jesus and His redeeming love, grace and mercy. Life really is ALL about JESUS. He is your answer to life and freedom.

Week Two, Day Three
Gaining Freedom over Temptation and Sin's Power.
Surrender is a Continual Process.

 Memory verse– Prov. 17:3 **The fining pot is for silver, and the furnace for gold: but the LORD trieth the hearts.**

As you are being conformed to the image of Jesus, you increasingly think in ways that are acceptable, thus pleasing to Him, because His Word is renewing your mind.

> **"You can't win the fight if you show up at the wrong arena."**
> - Ron Dunn.

As a believer, if you try to find freedom in any other way than a loving interaction with Jesus, you will not be in the right arena. Jesus is Truth and He makes you free in His Truth as your heart turns to Him.

Anyone who surrenderedly turns to Jesus to live in fellowship with Him has the assurance that sin will lose its controlling power over those areas where it once reigned. The more places of your mind that are brought under the control of Jesus, the more correctly you think and live.

Point of Truth: The Christian life is to be lived moment by moment in love for Christ!

If you try to fight against sin and temptation in the arena of inaccurate thoughts (thinking things that are not true), you will not win. If you try to win by focusing on doing better, keeping rules and laws, you will not win consistently. A wise thing to do when battling against sin is to saturate your mind with God's Word like a starving person would with food.

There may be times when sin does not have to release its grip until there has been a desperate, diligent turning and seeking of God. One day the disciples could not remove a demon from a child. When Jesus came, He sent the demon away. The disciples asked Jesus why they could not release the child? Mark 9:29 **And he said unto them, This kind can come forth by nothing, but by prayer and fasting.** It is not that we are in the same condition as the child (believers cannot be demon possessed) but we do battle with the same enemy. Sin will hold on to any place of control as tightly as it can. It is during such situations when **God wants to spend time with us.** That is what fasting and prayer are about, time spent in intimate fellowship with Jesus. He could have freed us from every stronghold immediately. It is not that any sin or the devil is so powerful that God has trouble sending them away. They flee when God tells them to do so.

Two possible reasons why God may not immediately free you from a stronghold may be: #1. You have not sought Him by taking the proper measures according to Biblical truth and guidelines (believed the truth, confessed and repented) thus, you have not taken deliberate actions of turning to God for pulling down strongholds).

#2. Jesus wants time with you. The time spent diligently seeking Him establishes your heart on Him. It takes time with Jesus to learn to love and treasure Him as one should.

Sin, the devil, and his forces are no stronger in one area against God than any other. The only reasons I can discover that God would hesitate to give freedom are either improper motives or inaccurate methods to freedom (actions not built on truth) or He wants some special time spent with you.

Prayer and fasting are good examples. God already knows what we need before we tell Him (Matt. 6:8). Both prayer and fasting fix our hearts on Jesus and through these we draw closer to Him and that is what He wants most of all.

Do you understand that God wants you for Himself? He wants your heart, your love. He has an ALL IMPORTANT PURPOSE for you (which we will explore in detail in coming lessons). He has promised to finish what He began in you (Phil. 1:6).

Job asked in Job 7:17 **What is man, that thou shouldest magnify him? and that thou shouldest set thine <u>heart</u> upon him?**

What has God set his heart (affection, care, desire and love) on according to Job 7:17? _____ God has set His heart on you. He wants you to set your heart (affection, care, desire and love) on Him in return.

1. Confess all known sins by name and refuse to participate in them any longer.
2. If there is a stronghold in your life, work through the steps in the previous lesson until you walk in freedom from sin's controlling power.

Strongholds may be in your mind because of abuses which happened without your consent, but, nonetheless, go through the process. You **do not have to replay the details of the sin in your mind and should not.** As soon as you recall a time when you committed a certain sin, go through steps of repentance and confession over each and every act of sin recalled. You may be surprised at how many past sins you committed that you will recall when confessing to break sin's control. You may remember acts of that sin that you have not thought of for years. It may take several periods of repenting and confessing to gain back the areas of your mind that were given to evil through sins. Each time you go through this process of repentance and confession, the Holy Spirit will be cleansing your mind and changing you more and more into the image of Jesus. You will experience more of His power and freedom as your mind is cleansed and renewed by the Holy Spirit, because a mind renewed increasingly understands that Jesus is God's answer and remedy for life and freedom.

Every time I am tempted to commit a sin that I cannot resist and be freed from in my mind, I strive to remember God's truth and ask Him to help me recall times where I yielded to that particular sin's temptation, and what lies I had believed about that sin. As I comprehend truth, I reject all false thinking and confess that sin by working through the steps mentioned.

I want my mind to be completely cleansed. (Although I know in this life one cannot be perfect, but one can and should desire and strive to be as sinless as possible). I do not confess the same act of sin (a particular event) over and over. Once I know I have confessed a particular act of sin, I am confident God has forgiven me and cleansed my mind, because He said He would if I would confess, 1 John 1:9 **If we confess our sins, he is faithful and just to forgive us *our* sins, and to cleanse us from all unrighteousness**.

Why recall and confess particular sins you have committed? By confessing sins, you build a fortress of truth in your mind that makes you know how damaging willfully committing sins can be. This works to help us strive to not put ourselves in future bondages and to grow in hating the things God hates.

As I recall a particular sin and go through the steps above, more areas of my mind are cleansed and renewed. I have come to know days and weeks of freedom from temptation in areas that once regularly plagued my mind. Again, I do not try to remember sins unless I am being overwhelmed by temptation in that area.

I once thought it was normal to be plagued with besetting temptations at various times. I thought it was just part of the old nature. I thought everyone had the same problem. I was wrong. My thinking was marred. Sin should never have a controlling, besetting, staining influence upon a believer's life. Jesus died and lives to make us free. By faith we can daily experience freedom in Him.

Thoughtfully read the following.

"Repentance is not a thing of days and weeks . . . to be got over as fast as possible. No, it is the grace of a lifetime, like faith itself . . . it is not true repentance which does not come to faith in Jesus and it is not faith that is not tinctured with repentance."— C. H. Spurgeon, Endnotes 10, p 204.

Evil forces or sin cannot take a place in a believer's mind unless he/she surrenders a place by sinning. It is through sins committed that sinful forces gain a dominating place of control. This is one reason why you must stop doing that particular sin or you will not gain freedom from the controlling power of that temptation. As long as you are participating in a certain sin, there will be no freedom from its dominating power.

Sin, in a believer's life, is like an illegal squatter that is discovered on someone's property. The squatter has no legal right to be there. Sin must be and can be driven out by reclaiming each place where its controlling influence is discovered. God's Word, His truth, is like a state's law and authority that gives a person the right to evict squatters from his/her property.

Romans 6:11 **Likewise reckon ye also yourselves to be dead indeed unto sin, but alive unto God through Jesus Christ our Lord. 12 Let not sin therefore reign in your mortal body, that ye should obey it in the lusts thereof.**

The focus of verse 11 is to "**reckon**" which means to think in line with truth, and that based on Jesus and Him alone. You are to **reckon** yourself dead to sin because, in the mind of God, you died with Jesus and when He arose, you did too. Your thinking must be all about Jesus and your new and powerful life in Him and His wonderful, purposeful life in you.

We are to disallow sin a place to reign in us by thinking truthfully about Jesus and devoting ourselves to Him, our new master. As verse twelve teaches, do not "**let**" sin dominate your life, and that because you died in Christ to your old master, sin, and you are now alive in your new master, Jesus.

"Faith never knows where it is being led, but it loves and knows the One Who is leading."
--Oswald Chambers, Endnote 10, p. 178.

Week Two, Day Four
Gaining Freedom over Temptation and Sin's Power.
God Made You for Himself.

 Memory verse– Prov. 17:3 **The fining pot is for silver, and the furnace for gold: but the LORD trieth the hearts.**

To gain the victory over sin's power, you must know the truth about God and yourself. Knowing God loves you and made you for Himself is the foundation of God's great and glorious work in you.

Have you asked questions like these: "Why am I on earth? Why did God create all of this? Why did He place me where I would hear the gospel and believe? What is my purpose for being here? Why has God kept me alive to this point? **What does God really want from me?** "

Is there any <u>thing</u> God needs you to do for Him that He cannot do without you? ____ Acts 17:24 **God that made the world and all things therein, seeing that he is Lord of heaven and earth, dwelleth not in temples made with hands; 25 Neither is worshiped with men's hands, as though he needed any thing, seeing he giveth to all life, and breath, and all things;** Is there any <u>thing</u> God cannot do by simply commanding it to be done?____ He created everything from nothing. Is there a church God could not have built if any of us had not been born? _____ Is there a person He could not reach if you were not here? _____ Could God have done everything you have been involved in through someone else or in some other way? <u>Yes</u>, and with less trouble than working with a person. Then why are you here? What can you do **for** God that He could not have without you? _____ I hope you wrote "nothing." There is one reason you are here that is above all others.

Point of Truth: God made you for Himself so He can have you in a love-driven relationship, out of which He with you and you with Him display His glory.

However, you can't display His glory as He wants until you know you are free from sins' controlling power. To God, you are a trophy of His grace, a product of His love and a theater of His Son's saving power.

You must know you are part of God's High Purpose, which is to give His Son a perfect, spotless bride that is fitted for Him. God started this incomprehensible work in you when He created you and then saved you for Himself. He is working in you to accomplish the things He has planned for you and those plans end with you being GLORIOUSLY transformed into His own likeness! Yes, YOU! God really does love you and He proved it when He gave His Son to save you and He will continue to show His love for and in you forever.

God's magnificent glory and love for you are to be the driving factors of your worship and celebration of Him, so get with worshiping and celebrating Him NOW in bold and fresh ways.

God could do all of the things you do <u>for</u> Him in many other ways without you, but He can't have you, without you. He can't have your heart treasuring His Son, unless He has you. He can't display His glory in you, without you. And that is why He made you as He did. He could have made you like a robot, programmed to say, "I love you God" and to do all things as He wills. But He didn't. He made you in His image. He gave you the power to make decisions. You can choose to treasure Jesus in love or not to. You can give your love, your heart, to whatever you choose.

Some saints have lived their lives without walking closely with Jesus with all of their hearts because they didn't know about keeping their hearts on Him or they simply treasured other things more than Him. And some have served Him for lesser reasons (such as, obligation, duty, pressure from others, etc); therefore, they did not live in intimate fellowship with Jesus and walk as closely with Him as they could have. Worship to them wasn't as important as other things because they didn't learn to love Him as they should have.

You don't have to turn your heart to Jesus and walk closely with Him. He won't force you to live with Him as your best friend, but He desires that you do. Jesus wants you to walk through each moment of life with Him. You are on earth for a short time by His appointment. Be sure to make the most of your time here. Don't waste the one and only life you have. Invest your life in love-driven intimacy in Him for whom you were created, Jesus.

Jesus can't be your intimate friend and companion without you.

Think about this: Jesus can't display His glory in an intimate friendship and companionship with Larry White without Larry White. Fill in the blanks with your name: Jesus can't have intimate companionship with _____ _____ without _____ and that is the reason He created me. Jesus created me for Himself. He created me to love and treasure Him, to walk with Him as His loving companion. He created me to display His glorious, life transforming power in this life and forever. He made me to share His life and likeness. He has predestined to eternally showcase His glory in me. YES ME! I am His and He is mine.

Read this paragraph again with your name in the blanks.

Colossians 1:16 **For by him** (Jesus) **were all things created, that are in heaven, and that are in earth, visible and invisible, whether they be thrones, or dominions, or principalities, or powers: all things were created by him, and for him.** How many things were "**created by him, and for him**?" _____ You are part of "**all things**." Jesus created you for Himself and what He wants most of all from you is you. He can't have you as He desires if He doesn't have your heart. He will not have you as He wants if you don't know why He created you. He created you for Himself, out of which comes all He wants to do in and through you. Make loving Jesus the reason for all you are striving to be and do and He will transform you.

Have you settled for things of this world while Jesus longs to be intimately in fellowship and companionship with you? _____ Why are you on earth?

I hope you wrote something like: "to lovingly, treasure Jesus as His companion so I can display His glory in this life and forever."

Jesus doesn't simply want you to do "Christian" things for Him, because "Christian" work can be done in ways and through motives that do not reveal His glory. When a believer does Christian things with a bad attitude, selfishly, pridefully, or for lesser reasons than loving Jesus, He does not display His glory due to Him as He could.

Love is a choice. You can choose to love anyone if you will to do so. To love God and others is a command. God would never command you to do something that He is not willing to work through you to accomplish.

God has done so many wonderful things for us because He is love. He created us and is working to bring us to dissatisfaction with all else but Himself and His glory.

There are at least three things which God desires from you that He cannot have without you and your heart:

1. <u>You</u>. If He doesn't have your heart, He doesn't have all of you.

2. <u>Intimate fellowship with you</u>.

3. <u>To demonstrate and display the glory due to His wonderful name through you</u>. The glory due to Jesus only happens when you are walking in close fellowship with Him. Revelation 4:11 **Thou art worthy, O Lord, to receive <u>glory and honour and power</u>: for thou hast created all things, and for thy <u>pleasure</u> they are and were created.** Why has God created **all things**?_____ God created you just like He wanted of His own good pleasure for His glory and honor. If your life is not lived for His glory, then you have wasted your life. Pray the following prayer:

Dear Father, open my understanding so I might see the wonderful things You have for me in Jesus. Help me see Him as He is so I will treasure Him so much that I count all things as nothing in comparison to Him.

Father, forgive me for my cold, departing heart. Turn my heart back to You. Have mercy upon me. You and You alone are the hope of life. There is no true and living God beside You;

Oh, GOD. I have resisted Your love while whoring after other loves. I have failed to consistently build my love for You on the foundation of Your love for me. Forgive me.

Oh my precious GOD, You have not allowed me to suffer because You enjoy seeing me hurt. My cries of disappointment have brought You no joy. You have allowed adversity seeking to shake me loose from all that would have my heart so You can have me for Yourself. You really do love me beyond my comprehension. In your love and goodness, You are pruning and purging my life. Your goal for me is for Your glory and my greatest good as Your Son's eternal companion. Wow!

You really do love me enough to continually work in me! You love me enough to let my plans fail, so I can better fit into your highest, purposeful plan, which is best. Oh dear LORD JESUS, thank You for dying for me. Thank You for sacrificing Yourself so I might really and actually live in daily fellowship with You. Your death was not in vain, dear Jesus. I give You all of my heart. I purpose to live for Your High Purpose. Glorify Yourself in me.

Father, now I see everything that has happened throughout my life, You are working together for my good and Your purpose-- Your Son's glory. All of the pain and disappointment; You are using to bring me to Your heart. Even my rebellion and sin which You hate, You have worked through it all seeking to have an intimate relationship of companionship with me. Thank You for loving me and wanting me to be Yours, and for wanting me to walk this through life and dwell in eternity with You. Amen.

"God is most glorified in us, when we are most satisfied in Him."
-John Piper, desiringgod.org

Week Two, Day Five
Gaining Freedom over Temptation and Sin's Power.
You are Free in Jesus to Obey His Will.

 Memory verse– Prov. 17:3 **The fining pot is for silver, and the furnace for gold: but the LORD trieth the hearts.**

John 8:32 **And ye shall know the truth, and the truth shall make you free. 33 They answered him, We be Abraham's seed, and were never in bondage to any man: how sayest thou, Ye shall be made free? 34 Jesus answered them, Verily, verily, I say unto you, Whosoever committeth sin is the servant of sin. 35 And the servant abideth not in the house for ever: but the Son abideth ever. 36 If the Son therefore shall make you free, ye shall be free indeed.** This passage discusses the fact that all who sin in a continual, habitual fashion are slaves to that sin (v. 34). In verse 36, Jesus used two different Greek words which are translated as "**free**." The first, (eleutheroo), means *to liberate*, or *to make free*. The second, (eleutherous), means *to liberate as a free citizen, thus no longer a slave*. So verse 36 could read: *If Jesus makes you free from the mastery of sin, you shall legally be at liberty to live as the free citizen you are in Him.*

True freedom is not doing as one pleases. It is having the liberty and power to do as one should. Citizens are free to do all that is within the parameters of the law of the land. Just as free citizens do not have the right to break the law without consequences, believers do not have the right to serve sin without consequences. Jesus not only did what was necessary to break sin's dominating power over us, He also set us at liberty when He defeated sin and death. He conquered our old sin master to make us free in Him, for Himself, so we can abide in a love-driven relationship with Him, out of which we strive for obedience to Him in all things.

A believer who does not know the truth of why Jesus wants to make him/her free, may become so discouraged and defeated that he/she may begin to believe all that can be obtained is a life of suffering, grief and bondage to a particular sin. A believer in such a state of mind does not believe he/she can be free. Patterns of habitual sinning have caused him/her to believe lies about having to have that sin. It is wrong to remain under the control of sin, because you now belong to Jesus and He wants you for Himself.

Point of Truth: It is unreasonable to believe that Jesus is calling you to follow Him without making you free to respond to His call.

Whatever Jesus calls you to be and do, He will empower you to accomplish, IF you interact with Him based on His love for you and your desire to love Him more.

If you want freedom from your sins so you can waste your life on yourself, He will not give it to you. He liberates you step-by-step so He can have more and more of you until He has all of you.

Jesus is calling you to a heart after Him. He won't flow fruitfulness through you while sin is flowing its corruption through you, because the fruit of sin is a willful lifestyle of sinning, which works against His High Purpose for you, which is His glory being revealed in you. Being mastered by sin is a life of bondage, misery and feelings of a wasted life, which is in contrast to His fruitful life of love, joy, peace and significance. You can't abide in two masters. You must choose Jesus and take action for love-driven obedience for the purpose of giving yourself more fully to Him.

Suppose you are in a prison cell and Jesus comes to visit you. He stands outside of your cell and tells you of His love for you and His plan to produce His fruit through you for His glory. Then He says, "Come walk with me in love." Do you think He expects you to get out of the prison cell by your own strength? He would not expect you to walk with Him until He had made you free. He knows you cannot follow obediently while sin has control over you. So, He legally presents full evidence that your sentence has been paid in full by Him and He defeated and conquered your former slave owner (sin). Therefore, He bought "YOU" to be His own possession for Himself, so you can have "HIM" as your very own. He did not free you from death so you can live for sin. He freed you so you can live for Him.

Some believers have mistakenly thought freedom means they are free to live as they want. In error, they make "grace" a license to do anything and live any way they choose. A believer is only free to lovingly live for Jesus as his/her Lord and Savior. As a person free in Christ you have the option to do wrong, but not the freedom to do wrong without consequences. Opting to do wrong or refusing to obey God's call results in chastisement. God disciplines you because of the damage sin does to intimacy with Jesus, out of which flow all He desires in and of you.

Jesus did all that is necessary to make you completely free in Him and for Him. In Jesus, you no longer have to give in to sin's temptation. You are free to refuse to practice any and every particular sin. I like to think of it as "As long as I am in my sinful flesh I will battle against sin, but, there is no particular sin I must commit." I am always free to say "no" to sin's temptations and that is what I am responsible to do out of love for Jesus.

My Journey with Anger and Freedom in Christ

For most of my life, including the first eighteen years as a pastor, I battled anger. I cannot recall when my temper first manifested itself. As a child I was often very angry and violent. I would do and say almost anything. I suffered much because of my anger.

I was saved at the age of nine. My anger and temper were not much different; I just felt worse about them. As I grew, I learned more of what I should be like and worked to become the person God wanted me to be. I wanted to walk closely with Jesus but I knew I wasn't doing very well, because of my failures in anger.

At age twenty, God called me to preach. I had been serving Him more faithfully than I ever had at that point. My anger wasn't a lot different, just more and more inside than out. So, less often was my anger visible. I knew I needed to change, but I didn't know how. (There is a big difference between being better at not sinning and being changed, thus, being victorious and free over sin's controlling power).

Point of Truth: The desire to change is part of God's work in changing you.

I sought God about my anger many times. I would confess and make commitments to Him about it. I would resolve to do better. And guess what? I did better. I learned to keep it inside so well that I even surprised myself, but I was not free, although I wanted to be. I hated it. What once was outward displays of anger became tension and twisting inside me. Although I refused to let anger have its way, I was often very frustrated throughout a day. But, as a pastor, I was "too holy" to let my anger show. I became good at controlling my outward anger. I could speak sweetly and smile while filled with frustration on the inside. I thought I had dealt with it. I thought I was victorious because I was doing so much better outwardly. Then God let me see that I was not free, because I can't love Jesus as He wants while I am frustrated and tense.

Anyone around me for awhile could see my frustration. One can only hide sin for so long. It always reveals itself somehow, and usually when you least expect it. I just grew to expect myself to always be that way. I felt like the answer was to continue holding my anger down, to discipline myself out of my problem.

My becoming better was the best I could do in my own strength. I wasn't victorious over anger, but I was doing the best I could. I **wanted to be** better and I was much better by keeping it inside. I hated my anger! I wanted to be a man of God more than anything. I simply **didn't know how** to change. I didn't know the victory I sought had already been won for me by Christ. I knew Jesus came and died for me in love, but I didn't know loving Him with my heart is God's path to my freedom. I was sure that if I were to overcome my anger and frustration, then I could draw nearer to Jesus and love Him more. However, drawing nearer to Him, loving Him more, was the way of gaining victory over my anger.

One night while watching my son play high school basketball, my anger revealed itself before I could get it under control. A referee grabbed my son's jersey and angrily pushed him backwards. Before I knew what had taken place, I was on the court. About the time he saw me (he could tell I was angry) I caught myself. I said to him, "That was my son; keep your hands off of him!" I went back and sat down. I was so ashamed. I felt I had betrayed Christ by displaying such an outburst of anger. I wasn't in control. Jesus wasn't in control. Anger was in control of me for that moment and I knew it.

That night several friends told me to not let it bother me; it was a parent thing. The head referee told the other man who had grabbed my son to apologize, and he did. As soon as the game ended, I went to the referee to apologize. He graciously accepted my apology. I wanted my family and friends to see me apologize. You see, I didn't want to bring a reproach to the name of Christ. I did not like my anger. I wanted to be a man of God. And for the most part, I was considered to be just that.

I knew what happened that night revealed my problem of anger's control in my life. I did not like the fact that anger had such control over me. My failure that night prompted me to turn to God. I searched His Word. I found I was supposed to be free in Christ. I already knew most of the verses that made claims of freedom. I had preached them for years, but I was not experiencing them. I had done better and thought that was the answer, but a careful searching of God's Word led me to see He wants more than me being better. He wants to change me. I was not changed. I was not conformed to His likeness (standing in the liberty of truth, free and victorious in His strength) I was only better than before, but not free. Inaccurate thinking caused me to believe I was okay because I was doing better, but God's Word opened my eyes.

God used the things that happened next to lead me to write this book. A couple of weeks before that outbreak of anger at the basketball game, I had heard a series of statements in a message about winning your child's heart.[4] I could not get away from thinking about those things. So, I began a word study in the Bible on the word "heart." It is used 830 times in the singular form and 113 times in the plural. I studied all 943 uses. After a few weeks of intense study, producing more than 100 pages of notes, God gave me His answer to my problem.

I clearly recall the day God made me free from anger. I was studying about my "heart" when I came to 2 Corinthians 3:15-18 my eyes were opened. 15 **But even unto this day, when Moses is read, the veil is upon their heart. 16 Nevertheless when it** (my heart) **shall turn to the Lord, the veil shall be taken away.** 17 **Now the Lord is that Spirit: and where the Spirit of the Lord is, there is liberty.** 18 **But we all, with open face beholding as in a glass** (mirror) **the glory of the Lord, are changed into the same image** (Jesus' image) **from glory to glory, even as by the Spirit of the Lord.** Suddenly, I understood what God wanted was saying to me. He wanted me to know when my heart turns to Him in full surrender, His Spirit gives liberty, freedom, by making me more like His Son, which includes: Free in Truth, Existing for His glory, A Compelling Example of High Character, One who Thinks Truthfully and Operates in Truth and Love by the power of His Spirit, etc. These are part of what it means to be made like Jesus.

In God's Word, I saw how the heart is His way of working genuine change in His children. I saw how the only true change, and not just getting better, had to come by God's own work. My part was to obey His call to turn to Him with all of my heart no matter the cost. Heartily following Jesus leads me into genuine change. That meant rejecting what I previously thought and replacing it with truth. What I needed more than anything was to turn my heart to Jesus, to treasure Him more than everything else. The big question was, and is today, who am I going to live for, who will have my heart, my love, myself or my Lord?

Point of Truth: Turning to Christ with all of your heart is the simplest, but most difficult decision you will ever make.

With 2 Corinthians 3:15-18 in mind, I read Romans 6:14 **For sin shall not have dominion over you: for ye are not under the law, but under grace.** I clearly saw when the heart turns to Christ, the Holy Spirit makes a believer free. At that point, I faced a decision. Did I believe God's Word to be true or not. I had always believed every word. Praise God, I believed! I dropped to the floor on my face before Him. I turned my heart to Jesus as best as I could. I confessed my sin and asked for His forgiveness. There on my face I knew I had turned. Thunder didn't roll, nor did lightning flash, but, something greater happened. The peace of God flooded my life. I was no stranger to the working of God's Spirit. Several times I had experienced His moving, working, and cleansing.

At times I had been at such a place of fresh spiritual renewal. My big question was, "Will it last?" As I studied God's Word, I saw how victorious Christians had hearts surrendered to Him. They walked with Him no matter the costs because they loved Him. As their hearts stayed on Him, they lived in victory because Jesus was flowing His life through them making them supernaturally fruitful for His glory. Many of them lived in His joy while being persecuted and some even put to death.

I now see all who were fruitfully victorious had learned to treasure Jesus more than anything, even their own lives. One surprising thing is they were as weak in their own strengths in many ways as I am. They messed up like I do. They battled their sins, like I do mine.

No! I can't live it. For years I tried. But, praise God, Christ can do nothing but live in victory over the world, the flesh, and the devil. Nothing is difficult for Him. I am not claiming perfection. I am far from perfect, but, I am now free from the dominating power of anger that once held me in bondage. That twisting tension that existed inside no longer controls me. I am at peace now in Jesus. Resting in Him, and that by His grace and mighty power working in me.

Because of my freedom in Jesus, there is not one sin I must commit. I do not have to serve sin and neither do you. I am free to choose to not give in to anger as I walk with Jesus with my heart after Him. I can choose to treasure Him more than what sin can give.

From that day I set out to test this new revelation. Guess what? I am living free from the bondage of anger. However, I have been tempted many times to let anger have its way in me again. As soon as I sense those stressful emotions of anger (that twisting tension inside that comes with fear and frustration) I run to Christ, asking for forgiveness, seeking Him with all of my heart. I regularly make a firm decision to give all fear, worry and other distractions to Him and strive to do all I can to trust He will see me through, and He does.

Again, I am learning to ask in each life situation, "God, what are you saying to me in this and how do you want me to respond?" These are what REALLY matter the most.

As I remain in the process of turning to Jesus, thus walking with Him with my focus on His love for me, He gives me freedom. I could choose to be angry again, and have been tempted to do so many times. I simply don't have to be angry any longer because Christ has done all that is needed for my freedom. My new Master, Jesus, broke the power of my old master, sin, (Romans 6) and now Jesus makes me free moment by moment.

Immediately, I began to preach this truth. Almost everywhere I preach this series of messages, God makes people free. During the first revival meeting where I preached these principles, a young man came to me and stated how he would like to have these principles in written form. He seemed so free, but yet so desperate. I knew how he felt. He was afraid it wouldn't last. I told him I was praying about writing this workbook. So that is partly how this work came about. What I have been sharing is not just a Bible study to me. It is the process that God has used, and uses everyday, to work freedom into my life. And, yes, it will last. The freedom will last as long as your heart is turned to Jesus and remains in that process, which is striving to abide in love-driven fellowship with Him. You do see Jesus is life don't you?

____ He is freedom and all we need to live free from the bondage of sin.

To explain the "Point of truth" above, I say turning to Christ is not difficult when you believe His Word. Actually, it is so simple that many will never see it. Many cannot get past thinking that pleasing God is a work of one's own strength, willpower, resolve and goodness. That is where I was for years. You see, turning from all you are to make a full surrender to Him is very difficult. It is death to your lordship over your life. Giving yourself, your heart, your affections, desires and loves, thus, control of everything to Jesus is a spiritual battle that your flesh does not want you to win. As long as I keep my heart focused on Jesus, He has my life and He is the one who makes me free. I can't free myself, but He can. My challenge is to make my life and love about Him, not myself.

Jesus doesn't want a place in your life, He wants to be your life. He doesn't even want first place, if that means you control all that remains. He is looking for people who will surrender fully to Him with all of their hearts. He is looking for those who will love and treasure Him more than anything.

All who treasure Jesus as we should, will experience Him and not simply something from Him. He is Revival. He is Life.

Don't make the mistake of focusing your life on your freedom, but rather, keep your attention on loving Jesus and you will live free in Him.

As the deer pants after the water brooks, so treasures, my soul after You, Jesus. My soul thirsts for God, for the living God: when shall I come to live with You forever in Your bright and glorious righteousness? (My paraphrase and comments of Psalm 42:1-2).

When I look for, or expect, praises from others, this reveals that I am not doing all as unto Jesus. How often I find myself in such a miserable state. God forgive me!

And ye shall seek me, and find me, when ye search for me with all your heart.
Jeremiah 29:13

Week Three, Day One
Keeping Your Heart on God.
Living a Changed Life.

 Memory verse– Col. 3:23 **And whatsoever ye do, do it heartily, as to the Lord, and not unto men;**

We have studied how and why the Holy Spirit makes you free when your heart turns to Jesus and remains in the process. Romans 6:14 **For sin shall not have dominion over you: for ye are not under the law, but under grace.**

Grace- God's favor toward you is totally unearned by you and can never be earned. His grace is 100% of His own nature.

It seems a person most often wants to do his/her own will, his/her own plans, and then ask God to place His blessing on them. That never works out in victory. It only leads to frustration, disappointment, disillusionment and guilt. To enter into the victory Jesus has won for us, we must seek Him to discover His will and then walk with Him in fulfilling it.

In this lesson you will see the practical application of how believers are to live and function in Christ as we go about our daily lives.

Colossians 3:16 **Let the word of Christ dwell in you richly in all wisdom; teaching and admonishing one another in psalms and hymns and spiritual songs, singing with grace in your hearts to the Lord. 17 And whatsoever ye do in word or deed, do all in the name of the Lord Jesus, giving thanks to God and the Father by him. 18 Wives, submit yourselves unto your own husbands, as it is fit in the Lord. 19 Husbands, love your wives, and be not bitter against them. 20 Children, obey your parents in all things: for this is well pleasing unto the Lord. 21 Fathers, provoke not your children to anger, lest they be discouraged. 22 Servants, obey in all things your masters according to the flesh; not with eyeservice, as menpleasers; but in singleness of heart, fearing God: 23 And whatsoever ye do, do it heartily, as to the Lord, and not unto men; 24 Knowing that of the Lord ye shall receive the reward of the inheritance: for ye serve the Lord Christ. 25 But he that doeth wrong shall receive for the wrong which he hath done: and there is no respect of persons.**

In verse 17 we see the command to live for Jesus in every way. 17 **And whatsoever ye do in word or deed, do ____ in the name of the Lord Jesus, giving thanks to God and the Father by him.** Does "all" mean everything you are responsible to do? _____ You are to do all that is right and your responsibility to do, in His name, thus for Him, as representing Him.

In verse 23 we are given the practical way to do everything in His name. 23 **And whatsoever ye do, do it heartily, as to the Lord, and not unto men;** ("**heartily**" implies affectionately, passionately), This one verse changes everything, because it changes our purposes for all we do.

Notice how this passage covers the major areas of life. Verses 15-16: Worship/Praise; Verses 18-21: Family; Verses 22-25: Service/job/School. Everything a believer is responsible to do is covered in this passage in some manner, because "**all**" includes everything.

Someone might say, "I know the things I am to do, but how can I be victorious as I do them?" "How can I live with my heart toward God?"
Point of Truth: Your heart's purpose and attitude, as you do what you are responsible to do, reflects the outcome.

If you start your job, service, or responsibility with a doing it ". . .

heartily, as unto the Lord, and not unto men" thus in a love for Him attitude and keep your heart toward Him, you will not be overcome by frustration or another evil. The word "**heartily**" (Col. 3:23) carries the idea of *from the soul, passionately*.

The more you learn to do **all** as unto Jesus, treasuring Him, the more freedom you will experience. Jesus is God's way for us to walk in victory over all things, including ourselves.

If you are struggling to be made free, turn your attention to Jesus and seek Him diligently and desperately. Go after Him passionately with all that is within you. Make Him the focus of your life no matter the cost.

Simply refuse to do anything you cannot do **as unto Jesus**. If it is wrong or questionable, don't do it. Treasure and love Jesus by doing all you are supposed to do ". . . heartily, as unto the Lord, and not unto men."

In the following, notice how Jesus connects loving Him and obeying Him. John 14:21 **He that hath my commandments, and keepeth them, he it is that loveth me: and he that loveth me shall be loved of my Father, and I will love him, and will manifest myself to him.**

John 14:23 **Jesus answered and said unto him, If a man love me, he will keep my words: and my Father will love him, and we will come unto him, and make our abode with him.**

You learn to love Jesus more deeply in direct proportion to knowing and believing His love for you. His love is revealed by all He has done, is doing and will do forever in and for you.

If you wait until you are overcome in temptation before you seek Him, before you call on Him, you have waited too long. Jesus doesn't want to be the last place you go. He wants to be the center of your attention. He wants to be the first one you think of in times of temptations and troubles, as He wants to be the first one you think of in times of blessings and honor.

To narrow the gap between where you are spiritually and God's great and high plan for your life, you must learn to do everything as unto Jesus for His glory. Jesus being glorified in you and you being free in Him so you can give yourself to Him in every way is the summit of God's purpose for your life. There is no greater reason to live than to live for Jesus in love-driven communion with Him.

You will more intensely strive to do all things with fortitude, passion and crowning effectiveness, when doing them for Jesus because you have discovered His love and purpose for you, which are glorious. You are at your best when you do everything just for Him. Living as unto Jesus makes your life the best it can be. It changes your attitude because your affections are not on things of this earth, but rather, set on things above (Col. 3:1-2).

Treasuring Jesus is where your life flows toward His life in all you are and do. Such interaction with Jesus causes your sacrifices for Him to touch His heart in the deepest ways. Your sacrifices of love for Him are torrents of joy flowing to Him. God really does delight in those who love Him.

Sometimes a believer will ask if a "questionable" thing (something not spoken to directly in the Bible) is right or wrong. I usually respond by saying, "Can you honestly do that '**heartily**, in expressions of love, as unto Jesus' or is it something you know you cannot? There is your answer. Be honest before God and He will teach you what is right and wrong. If you are being deceived, He will reveal that to you as you focus on Him. Any and everything you do can be evaluated by asking yourself, "Can I do this heartily, affectionately as unto my Lord Jesus."

Week Three, Day Two
Keeping Your Heart on God.
Don't Confuse Forgiving Others with Reconciliation.

 Memory verse– Col. 3:23 **And whatsoever ye do, do it heartily, as to the Lord, and not unto men;**

When God seeks to change or purify your life, He simply, but powerfully, calls you, your attention unto Himself. He does this through His Word, His Spirit, circumstances (good or bad), relationships (especially very important ones) and through your heart. When God calls you to His heart, there will be a lack of peace until you draw close to Him in response to His love. This lack of peace serves as a summons to seek Him more diligently.

To bring about greater growth, God may allow some difficult things to touch your life. Adversities are calls from God for you to humbly flee to Jesus for refuge and help as you strive to get as right with Him as you possibly can.

Often, before God does significant things in and through us, He allows us to go through some difficult and trying things, whereby we are drawn to a deeper walk with Jesus, out of which we do greater works.

The shepherd boy, David, fought bears and lions while alone in the wilderness and defeated them because he practiced spending intimate time with God in private devotion. Later, God used him to defeat Goliath in public. Don't run from adversity when you know your heart is fixed on Jesus. Run to Jesus and know and believe He loves you!

David prayed: Psalm 139:23 **Search me, O God, and know my heart** : (motives, desires, affections, thus, what my life is about) **try me, and know my thoughts:** Are my thoughts aligned with His Word, [accurate and established in truth], or is there some lie which I have accepted that is working against my walk with Jesus? 24 **And see if there be any wicked way in me, and lead me in the way everlasting.**

God does not require us to be sinlessly perfect before we can abide in Him, or none of us could. However, He does require us to turn to Jesus in such a way that we strive to do all we know we should to please Him, to be as right as we can be, because we love and treasure Him that much.

Suppose I am not sensing God's conviction, but then I remember a guy who hurt me and I have a bitter, unforgiving, spirit toward him. I must turn at that point. My own desire may not be to forgive, but my desire to be right with Jesus overrides my selfish desire, so I forgive, because His desires have become my desires. I forgive others not because I always first want to do so and not because I am a "good" person, but because Jesus wants me to forgive. I'm not good enough to do right on my own. I can honestly say Jesus makes the difference between the bondage I once lived in and the freedom I now have. The reason I came to forgive is because God called me to Himself. He did this by not allowing my life to work out in peace and effectiveness while I was not heartily focused on His Son. I know I cannot live effectively without being right with Him, which includes forgiving offenders. So, His righteous desires replace my selfish desires, then I want to forgive and I do.

As I turn to Jesus with all of my heart, treasuring Him more than anything, the Holy Spirit helps me freely forgive. If I do not forgive, that is evidence my heart has not turned to Jesus in full surrender, thus my love for Him is not as it should be. A lack of forgiveness (or continuing in any sin) reveals how I am more concerned about my will than I am Him.

Check the memory verse. You cannot commit sin "**heartily, as to the**

Lord." Failure to do right shows you care more about your selfish wants than you care about walking closely with Jesus.

Some say, "I know I need to forgive. I have tried, but I can't." They can't if they follow selfish desires. They can't with their hearts set on anything other than Jesus. And, if you forgive through your power, you will take the credit. But, if you forgive because Jesus wants you to, He will get the credit. It is a lie to say you cannot do what God commands. The truth is, with Jesus flowing His life through you, you can do everything He asks. Philippians 4:13 **I can do all things through Christ which strengtheneth me.**

World changing, life transforming obedience is driven by love in response to Jesus, and that by focusing on His love for you. If you love Him, you will obey Him (John 14:21-23). If you do not obey, it is likely He will allow adversity in your life to awaken you to your need for Him. (Although, not all adversity is because of disobedience).

Point of Truth: Loving Jesus more (in response to His love for you) is the avenue to you doing everything He is calling you to do.

The bondage of an unforgiving spirit is one of the worst types. It sours all of life. Bitterness hurts the bitter person far more than anyone else. An unforgiving spirit is unlike Jesus. Someone said, "Bitterness is like you drinking poison and expecting it to hurt your offender."

Remember, God is working to change each believer into the likeness of Jesus. He is working to narrow the gap between what you are now and all He wants you to be for His Son's glory. Therefore, be wise and work with Him.

At times, a reason Christians think they can't forgive is because they confuse forgiving with being reconciled to an offender. There are times when reconciliation is not possible, nor reasonable, because the offender will not reconcile, or the person cannot be located, or the person has died, or the offender has proven he/she cannot be trusted, therefore, he/she might further abuse the one desiring reconciliation.

Forgiveness and reconciliation are different things. It has been said, "Forgiveness is what one person does in his/her own heart. Forgiving an offender is between you and God. Reconciliation is between you and your offender. It only takes one person to forgive. Reconciliation takes two persons." Start with forgiveness and leave reconciling to God until He gives you the opportunity to seek reconciliation. Do what you can to reconcile as God in His time allows, but forgive now.

You can forgive anyone who has hurt you by loving Jesus enough to do so. You may not want to, but you can forgive by choosing to treasure Jesus more than yourself and your feelings.

Learn to love Jesus more by turning your heart to Him in response to His love for you, and you will be amazed who you can love and forgive. If you need to forgive someone, the gap that now exists between you and God's will can be overcome by making Jesus the object of your heart and love. Forgiving those who have hurt you is not easy, but getting to walk in close fellowship with Jesus is worth the costs. Let Him see how much you believe He loves you by forgiving your offenders. The more difficult it is to forgive, the more pleasure God has in you when you forgive, because by forgiving, you glorify His Son. Read 1 John 4:16 (in the box on the right).

Some might ask, "What about Matthew 5:23 **Therefore if thou bring thy gift to the altar, and there rememberest that thy brother hath ought against thee; 24 Leave there thy gift before the altar, and go thy way; first be reconciled to thy brother, and then come and offer thy gift.**" This

> 1 John 4:16
> **And we have known and believed** the love that God hath to us. God is love; and he that dwelleth in love dwelleth in God, and God in him.

passage speaks to times when the one who has come to worship is the offender, not the one needing to forgive an offender.

1. Read 1 John 4:16 again and ask God to increase your understanding of His love for you.
2. Has God reminded you of the need to forgive someone? _____ If so, on a separate sheet, write a prayer of forgiveness. (You may want to destroy it after writing it). Open up to God and allow Him to purge your heart and replace that bitterness with a greater love for Jesus.
5. Pray for the leaders in your family, government, your local church family, and all other persons God has placed over you.

Forgiving offenders is a continual exercise of faith in God. Actually, in ALL of the Christian life, faith must override one's feelings for faith to operate as it should. Living by faith doesn't mean you always FEEL strong and effective in life. As a matter of fact, when you feel weak and overwhelmed with a sense of insufficiency in yourself to be the person God wants, but yet, you strive in love-driven pursuit of Jesus, you become a theater for God to show the power of His grace to you and others. Your part is to believe and trust Jesus by leaning on, and freshly surrendering to, Him each time your feelings try to draw you away from faith in Him. By faith, you learn to trust God no matter your circumstances, especially when your feelings tell you something other than God is for you. Romans 8:31 **What shall we then say to these things? If God be <u>for us</u>, who can be against us?** When your feelings want you to attack or degrade yourself or others, or give up in defeat, or question God's love for you, don't succumb to such temptations, but rather, know God is at work and He will bring you through, even if what you face takes you home to heaven to be with Him.

> 2 Corinthians 12:9 **And he said unto me, My grace is sufficient for thee: for my strength is made perfect in weakness. Most gladly therefore will I rather glory in my infirmities, that the power of Christ may rest upon me. 10 Therefore I take pleasure in <u>infirmities, in reproaches, in necessities, in persecutions, in distresses</u> for Christ's sake: for when I am weak, then am I strong.**

Read 2 Corinthians 12:9-10 (in the box) and notice how God spoke of Paul's adversities and His grace that made Paul strong. Paul became strong in the power of God when he viewed his infirmities (weaknesses and painful things) as there to serve him, by keeping him humbly dependent on Jesus.

The underlined words describe every difficulty and the helpless feelings that come with living in a human body. Your weaknesses and adversities make you feel unimportant, useless, weak, and feeling ashamed because you are so weak. Your weaknesses are by God's design. God made this world in such a way to cause us to constantly realize how deeply we need Him. Every trial, difficulty and adversity should drive you to forsake self-sufficiency, so you will fully rely on Him. Determine now to live victoriously in the reality of your insufficiencies, pains and hurts, (that you can't change, and that God has chosen not to change) by desperately depending on Jesus alone.

If you have feelings of inadequacy and insufficiency to be the person God wants, thus to live a life of significance, then you are in the perfect place for your faith to "show up" and for Jesus to "show out" in you. It takes recognized weakness to reveal to you how you can't make your life work without living in constant dependence on Jesus. You are nothing when it comes to living your life by your strength and personal fortitude. However, in Jesus, you are more than a conquer as you love and depend on Him. (Read Romans 8:35-37, in the box). Our lives in this world are like sheep being killed all day long. You need Jesus every moment, so live like it.

> Romans 8:35 **Who shall separate us from the love of Christ? shall tribulation, or distress, or persecution, or famine, or nakedness, or peril, or sword? 36 As it is written, For thy sake we are killed all the day long; we are accounted as sheep for the slaughter. 37 Nay, in all these things we are more than conquerors through him that loved us.**

You can triumph in your life, **in Christ**, even though you exist in this fallen world of trials and adversities, **IF** you will live in conscious awareness of your need for Him. Your weaknesses consistently reveal how much you need Jesus, the only one who can make your life significant.

Week Three, Day Three
Keeping Your Heart on God.
Living for God's High Purpose.

 Memory verse– Col. 3:23 **And whatsoever ye do, do it heartily, as to the Lord, and not unto men;**

We are studying about how to keep our hearts on Jesus as we go through each day so we can fruitfully walk with Him in heart to heart fellowship. Ephesians 6:5 **Servants, be obedient to them that are your masters according to the flesh, with fear and trembling, in singleness of your heart, as unto Christ; 6 Not with eyeservice, as menpleasers; but as the servants of Christ, <u>doing the will of God from the heart</u>; 7 With good will doing service, as to the Lord, and not to men: 8 Knowing that whatsoever good thing any man doeth, the same shall he receive of the Lord, whether he be bond or free.**

Although these verses were addressed to Christian slaves, verse eight says they are for all believers, "**bond or free.**"

I hope you are developing a pattern of doing everything you do "**heartily, as unto the Lord, and not unto men.**" The more you practice doing everything as unto Jesus, the more freedom you experience.

According to Ephesians 6:5, how are we to do our work? "5 . . . in ____ _____ **as unto Christ.**" The word "**singleness**" means just that, for no other purpose. We are on earth for Jesus and His purposes. Our purpose for everything must be unto Him.

God is raising up a generation of believers who love and serve Jesus with all of our hearts. We are learning to treasure Him far above all else. If you are not, will you become one?

Jesus wants us to do all "as to Him" for His glory and our good. There has never been a better time to be a good example of treasuring Jesus enough to strive to sacrificially obey Him. Your world needs to see you really do believe and live in the security of knowing God loves you. The people in your world need to see your faithfulness to Jesus because you love Him in response to His love for you.

The spiritual enemies of our souls fight to keep us from living with our hearts fixed on Jesus. They do all they can to get us to question God's unchanging love for us. They tempt us to doubt God's love, because they know Personal Revival (spiritual renewal) takes place when we believe God loves us unconditionally, because He does. Our spiritual enemies know our response to His love is that we turn to Jesus with all of our hearts, by which He changes us and expands His kingdom.

Many Christians are defeated because their hearts are not fixed on Jesus. Suppose a snake bites a defeated Christian (consider the snake like sin and failure). What many do is pick up a mental club and instead of hitting the snake, they hit themselves. They tell themselves: "If I were better, snakes wouldn't bite me. I must be terrible or there is something in my past which God is holding against me and the curse from it is a miserable life." What we need to do to overcome an attitude of defeat is to receive God's grace and truth, to believe He loves us, while refusing to think things that are not true.

When you surrender yourself to God, the power of God flows through you to accomplish His will in you. You surrender to God's grace by consciously and heartily doing all as unto Him, and not for any other reason.

God tells how His grace helped Paul do his ministries. Romans 1:3 **Concerning his Son Jesus Christ our Lord, which was made of the seed of**

David according to the flesh; 4 **And declared** *to be* **the Son of God with power, according to the spirit of holiness, by the resurrection from the dead:** 5 **By whom we have received** grace **and apostleship,** for obedience to the faith among all nations, **for his name:** Paul was given God's grace for obedience to the faith among all nations, for Jesus' name.

Paul also spoke of God's grace that was lavishly bestowed upon him so he could accomplish God's will in 1 Corinthians 15:9 **For I am the least of the apostles, that am not meet to be called an apostle, because I persecuted the church of God. 10 But by the grace of God I am what I am: and his grace which** *was bestowed* **upon me was not in vain; but I labored more abundantly than they all: yet not I, but the grace of God which was with me.** When you do your daily responsibilities **heartily, as to the Lord, and not unto men,** you can do them with patience and effectiveness by receiving God's **grace** to help you behave as you should.

If you have not, will you turn your heart to Him and obey, while looking to Him to help you by His grace? _____ When you know your heart is driven by love for Jesus, you can expect His favor, His help, His grace to be freely given to you.

Each time I preach from this series of messages, I challenge the listeners to write out Col. 3:23 and memorize it and to post it at every place where they have responsibilities which tend to bring resentment or frustration.

Who have you been living for? If you are living for your family, that won't get it done. If you are merely working for your employer for a pay check, that is not God's high purpose for your life. Begin to live, work and play as unto the Lord Jesus. Live FOR HIM in everything.

Have you been hitting yourself because of failures or failed expectations in your life? _____ If you have, stop hitting the wrong one. Run to your best friend, Jesus, the One Who loves you more than anyone. Flee to Him with all of your heart and tell Him what the enemy has been doing to you. James 4:7 **Submit yourselves therefore to God. Resist the devil, and he will flee from you.** 8 **Draw nigh to God, and he will draw nigh to you. Cleanse your hands, ye sinners; and purify your hearts, ye doubleminded**. A pure heart is one of singleness in purpose to Christ. Anything that is of one substance is pure. It may be pure iron, gold, etc. God says, "**purify your hearts**" as you "**draw nigh**" to Him. Develop a heart of one type, which is a heart for Jesus. Stand firmly on His Word and refuse to believe all lies. Believe the Truth! Romans 6:14 **For sin shall not have dominion over you: for you are not under the law, but under grace.** Your obedience is not a law to keep. It is a life with Jesus that you are now free to live in Him and His love.

You do not live based on law. You are in God's grace, so function every moment based on His love and favor toward you, which is fully based on His goodness and love, not yours.

1. Should sin have dominion over you? _____
2. Seeing sin should not have dominion over a believer, is every believer experiencing a life of freedom from bondage? _____ Many are not because they do not **know** God loves them or the truth concerning the victory that is already theirs in Christ. Or, they have not turned their hearts to Him and remained in the process, thus, they are not striving to treasure Jesus above all and doing everything "**heartily as unto Him**." Or, they have not learned to look unto Jesus when the enemy and temptation attack (Heb. 12:2-4).
3. If you tend to blame others or yourself when things go wrong, pray the following: "Father, by faith in You and Your Son, give me Your grace to

KNOW YOU LOVE ME and to no longer mentally hit myself or others when I face trials. Help me remember to run to Jesus with all of my heart as my only refuge and strength. Help me find the comfort I need in Jesus as I learn to cherish Him more deeply. Help me take full responsibility for my own sins and failures. Please renew my mind and transform my life through Your Word and by Your Spirit, as I repent, confess and sacrificially strive to obey Your will. Thank You for loving me and working in me to make me like Jesus. Amen."

4. Write a responsibility that you do where you tend to find yourself fearful, anxious, resentful, tense or frustrated._____

5. Spend some time in prayer giving yourself fully to Jesus asking Him to help you do all as unto Him.

6. If you are experiencing freedom, share with someone today about the wonderful friend you have in Jesus.

7. Praise God for His love, greatness, mercy, and grace.

8. Seek to take someone who does not attend worship with you at the next appointed time.

The following passage speaks to a most important thing concerning gaining the victory Jesus has for us. 2 Corinthians 10:3 **For though we walk in the flesh, we do not war after the flesh: 4 (For the weapons of our warfare are not carnal, but mighty through God to the pulling down of strong holds;) 5 Casting down <u>imaginations</u>, and every high thing that exalteth itself <u>against</u> the knowledge of God, and <u>bringing into captivity every thought to the obedience of Christ;</u>**

Most people, if not all, must to do battle with incorrect thoughts. The world, the flesh and the devil and his forces say things to us that are not true. They try to get us to believe and function is an arena of self-degrading thoughts. They say things like "you're dumb," or "you're stupid," or "you're ugly," or "you're too short or too this or that" etc. They do this based many times of what other persons in our lives have said to us or about us. They like for us to replay in our minds the worse things that we have been told or that we have perceived about ourselves.

We must reject such "stinking thinking" or we will not win. The forces of darkness will speak all kinds of lies into your mind in an attempt to try to get you to believe inaccurate things about yourself, others and God.

They will try to convince you that God is against you. That He is holding your past failures against you, and such things as this. Those voices are lies and filled with deceptive, destructive purposes. You must reject their purposes and replace them with God's purposes, which are truly amazing.

Recently, I spoke with a brother in Christ who told me how as a child his dad was an angry man. He told of how his dad often told him he was "stupid and couldn't do anything right." He is now in his fifties. He told how every time he makes a mistake in life (which is regularly, like all of us) he hears those destructive words. He spoke of how he has heard those words in his mind for all of his life and has to deal with them each time he struggles in any way.

You may be in a similar place in your life. Please know that "in Christ" you are not the same person as before and should not continue to believe degrading lies. Jesus didn't save you to degrade you. He saved you for His High Purpose, which is to show how powerful His Son's saving power really is and when He gets finished with you, you will display His grace and glory in splendorous ways beyond what we can't ever imagine in this life.

Week Three, Day Four
Keeping Your Heart on God.
Prayer and God's High Purpose.

 Memory verse– Col. 3:23 **And whatsoever ye do, do it heartily, as to the Lord, and not unto men.**

Today we will study an exciting truth about prayer and GOD'S HIGH and ALL IMPORTANT PURPOSE for you. As you walk through each day with Jesus, you talk to Him and He communes with you. Conversation is an important part of fellowship and heartfelt communication helps develop intimacy.

As you pray, the Holy Spirit makes intercession for you concerning your needs and requests (even when you don't know what to ask or how to word your prayer). Romans 8:26 **Likewise the Spirit also helpeth our infirmities:** -(weaknesses) **for we know not what we should pray for as we ought: but the Spirit itself maketh intercession for us with groanings which cannot be uttered. 27 And he that searcheth the hearts knoweth what is the mind of the Spirit, because he maketh intercession for the saints according to the will of God.**

The Greek word translated "**helpeth**" (v. 26) means *to take hold of the opposite together.* As soon as you begin to talk to God (even though you may not feel secure in knowing how to pray effectively and correctly) as you pray, the Holy Spirit takes *hold of the opposite end* of your requests, and intercedes for you, and works to fulfill the Father's will for your good. Doesn't it bring joy to know the Holy Spirit has ahold of the other end of your requests and works in you each time you pray? ____ And, as you pray, God works in you in special ways, as we shall see.

Faithfulness in praying should **not** be built on feelings of effectiveness, because many times you may not feel effective. Faithfulness in praying should be built on God's promises, His Word, regardless of how you feel.

The key to an effective prayer life is obedience in asking, seeking, and knocking in prayer and not giving up. To talk with God as He wants, you must know He loves you and He has a high purpose for you and your prayer life is part of His work in you and in the world. Every person God uses to touch His world in extraordinary ways are persons of consistent prayer. This is no coincidence. Prayer is a key element of His work of refining and anointing a person in powerful ways.

Praying faithfully and being used supernaturally sounds too simple to be true, but it is. If you don't lift your desires, needs, and the needs of this world in prayer, the Holy Spirit will not intercede for you in the special way that He does when you pray, thus, you will not be used as powerfully in His kingdom as you could be. If you do faithfully pray with confidence in God, you can know the Holy Spirit is working with you in powerful ways.

It is no accident that persons who have been mightily used of God were persons of consistent and extraordinary faithfulness in prayer.

Notice verse 27. My paraphrase: "*When you are praying, the Father searches your heart (examines your motive to see why you are asking), and He knows what the Holy Spirit has in mind for you, because the Holy Spirit has told the Father by interceding for you as you made your request.*" At least two things happen when you are praying. First, the Father examines your motives ("**searcheth the hearts**") and secondly, He examines His will for you, which the Holy Spirit works to fulfill as He makes **(intercession for you according to the will of God)**. With these two actions at work, He answers your prayers. But the outcome of The Holy Spirit's special intercession for you doesn't end there.

Your prayer life, thus, The Holy Spirit's intercession for you, is the light into which the powerful verse, Romans 8:28 is given, **And we know that all things work together for good to them that love God, to them who are the called according to his purpose.** The first word "**And**", ties it directly to the thoughts of verse 27. Along with knowing the Holy Spirit helps us when we pray, verse 28 states (my paraphrase with comments) *"And we also know all things that have happened to us, or will ever happen to us, are being worked together for our good, because the Holy Spirit is always interceding for us to fulfill God's will. We must know God does these things to fulfill His High and ALL IMPORTANT PURPOSE."*

The big question at this point might be, "What has God planned for me and what is His **purpose**?" I can assure you that no one knows all He is going to use to get each one to His final purpose. But, we are told what that final purpose for every believer is. It's in verse 29 **For whom he did foreknow, he also did predestinate to be conformed to the image of his Son, that he might be the firstborn among many brethren.** The word "**that**" is a purpose statement. It could read "**so that.**" God's ultimate purpose for everyone who believes is to conform him/her to the **image of Jesus so that he might be the firstborn among many brethren.**

Therefore, when you pray, God takes your request and answers so all He does works together with all things to fulfill His ultimate plan for His Son's life to be formed in you. Galatians 4:19 **My little children, of whom I travail in birth again until Christ be formed in you.** God's plan is for you to think, live and be like Jesus Christ in mind and purpose, because His life is in you and you are being transformed into His likeness so **that HE MIGHT BE the firstborn among many brethren.** Your life is all about Jesus from God's perspective, plan and purpose, so He is working all things together to make you like Him.

God will let you have some things and experiences that He will not give to others. He will give others things and experiences that He will not give to you. Why? Because He has different plans to get each of us to His one, ultimate purpose, which is, every believer being **conformed to the image of His Son**, for the High **Purpose** of Jesus having a loving family of brothers and sister, of which He is the **firstborn**. His plan is to make you shine with the brightness of His character, redeeming power and glory forever.

We know prayer is one of the most important things we can do. Many of the most clear and wonderful promises of God are related to obedience in prayer. Yet, prayer gets little attention in many believers' lives.

What Satan fears the most is a praying saint, especially one who understands God's ultimate purpose for his/her life.

Jesus spoke of the impact of your prayer life in John 15:7 as it relates to you abiding in Him. **If ye abide in me, and my words abide in you, ye shall ask what ye will, and it shall be done unto you.**

1. Write one burden of your heart that you would like to know God is working on with you. _____

Pray and tell God that you believe His Word, which declares He is working all things for your good to show Jesus really is **the firstborn of many brethren**, and He has the power to transform each one into His own, glorious likeness.

I wrote earlier "God's will in you has more to do with you being changed than the things He does through you." I say this because the most important thing is **you** being **changed** into **Jesus'** likeness for His glory. So prayer isn't only to get things done in our world for God's glory. Prayer is an important part of God's plan to change your life now and forever, and that, for the eternal display of His Son's glory. This should compel us to pray more.

God is determined to show Jesus really is sufficient to save and transform sinners like us into **called**, **justified** and ultimately **glorified** saints (v.30), thus the **firstborn** of many brothers and sisters and that all by His sacrificial life and death. Some day soon, we will exist in His glory in heaven forever. Picture in your mind, you with Jesus as His own in heaven and you without spot or blemish, robed in His righteousness, shining in His glory. Shouldn't we work diligently to show His glory now in all we are and do? Romans 8:30 **Moreover whom he did predestinate, them he also called: and whom he called, them he also justified: and whom he justified, them he also glorified.**

In the predestined purposes of God, every believer is already **called**, **justified** and **glorified**. Soon we will have in our experience all He has predestined for us, and that for His High Purpose of Exalting His Son.

"I discovered that prayer is not a religious exercise--it is a human necessity."
-Ron Dunn, Endnote 6, p. 6.

Pride says you can live your life effectively without spending time in prayer. Humility says you can't. It is the same for we who lead our Lord's churches, prayer is a necessity. Jesus said, Matthew 21:13 **. . . It is written, My house shall be called the house of prayer; . . ..**

If our nation is to be granted Revival and Spiritual Awakening, we must return to God in prayer. And the same is true concerning working with God to change us to exalt His Son in us.

Two things that will have the most impact upon you as you strive to live a pure, love-driven life for Jesus are memorizing His Word and praying consistently.

If you struggle to memorize, pick one verse and work on it and you will find you can retain the truth, the concepts, that God states in that verse. And set a time, with a list of prayer needs, and strive to be faithful in praying in a simple, regular, conversational way. Talk to God openly and heartily. He already knows your need to be changed and has purposed to finish what He has begun in you (Phil. 1:6) which is to make you like His Son.

If I regard iniquity in my heart, the Lord will not hear me: Psalm 66:18

Week Three, Day Five
Keeping Your Heart on God.
God's High Purpose and Loving Others.

 Memory verse– Col. 3:23 **And whatsoever ye do, do it heartily, as to the Lord, and not unto men.**

It is exciting to know that God has predetermined to conform each believer into the **image of His Son**, thus to be trophies of His grace to display His Son's glory now and forever.

Now, let's see more about WHY God made this a great promise. Romans 8:29 **For whom he did foreknow, he also did predestinate to be conformed to the image of his Son, <u>that he might be the firstborn among many brethren</u>.** I know of no stronger word to express God's promise to complete the work He began in us than the word "**predestinate.**" Before God created the world, He (God the Father, God the Son and God the Holy Spirit) decided thru Jesus to reveal His glory to all high forms of created life (human and other spiritual beings). All of creation points directly to God and His glory. In simple terms, the word **predestinate** means whatever God has decreed, He will bring to pass as He wants.

The reason God has predestined to conform all who believe into the image of His Son is **that he might be the firstborn among many brethren.** God's goal of Jesus being **the firstborn among many brethren** is to demonstrate His Son's matchless love and power to save and transform a life, and these for His glory.

The Holy Spirit is working in you for the purpose of accomplishing for Jesus everything God the Father promised He would do for His Son in everyone He redeems. He is working in you to make you ready to dwell eternally with Jesus as His glorious bride.

God says He saved us by His grace through faith for His purposes. His Highest Purpose, the one that absorbs all others, is stated emphatically in Ephesians 2:7 **That in the ages to come he might shew the exceeding riches of his grace in his kindness toward us through Christ Jesus.**

Point of Truth: You are and will forever be a trophy of God's grace, so strive to live like it. Rom. 8:29 does not say "that you might be" something. It says, "**that he might be . . . .**"

Point of Truth: God's work in <u>you</u> is more about <u>you</u> than the <u>things</u> you do for Him and His work in <u>you</u> is much more about <u>Jesus</u> than it is you.

You are part of God's plan to display the extraordinary, marvelous, life-transforming power of His Son's life in you. This is why God only accepts us in His Son by His own righteousness, thus there can be no merit on our part in salvation. ITS ALL ABOUT JESUS! God does not want us thinking we are earning any part of our acceptance with Him in salvation. He wants us to know His Son gets all of the credit and glory for saving us and transforming our lives. So, we must know God's Highest Purpose for creating and saving us is so we can join Him in His work for Jesus' glory. We do this by living and doing all things for Jesus in a love-driven pursuit of Him. (For more insight about God's High Purpose, read very carefully Ephesians 1:3-14 and Ephesians chapter 3).

The following passage was spoken by Jesus to His disciples after He had stressed the importance of "**abiding in Him**" (John 15:4-7). The practical application of "**Abiding**" in Jesus is what I call "keeping your heart turned to Jesus or treasuring Him above all things, because the way we abide is with our hearts focused on Him and His love for us. Then Jesus said, John 15:11 **These things have I spoken unto you, that my joy might remain in you, and that your joy might be full. 12 This is my commandment, That ye love one another, as I have loved you.** And verse, 17 **These things I command you, that ye love one another.** Almost in the same breath as Jesus spoke about **your joy**, He commands you to **love one another, as** He has **loved you**.

John 15:9 **As the Father hath loved me, so have I loved you: continue ye in my love.** What does it mean to "**continue**" in Jesus love? It means to relate to Him in a love-driven relationship. Loving Him is the only acceptable basis of WHY you are to strive to **keep** His **commandments**. Jesus loves you and wants you to display your love for Him in all you do.

10 **If ye keep my commandments, ye shall abide in my love; even as I have kept my Father's commandments, and abide in his love.** Jesus didn't cause His love for His Father by keeping His commandments, He displayed it. And, you can't cause your love for Jesus by keeping His commandments either, but you can show you really do love Him by keeping them.

Your life stands as a test so you can evaluate if you are truly abiding in Christ, thus, loving and treasuring Him as you should or if you are not. Striving in loving others and obeying all God commands are indicators of how deeply you treasure Jesus in your heart. Write what you think God is saying in Luke 6:46 **And why call ye me, Lord, Lord, and do not the things which I say?** _____

_____

At times, I have wished that my fellowship with Jesus was between me and Him alone. When I have been offended, I do not always want to forgive simply for my fellowship with that person to be restored. But, when I seek to walk in fellowship with Jesus and remember I have not done all I could to forgive someone, I am required to forgive and I want to forgive because I want to please my Lord much more than I want to remain bitter. I want to show my love for Jesus by doing the things He wants me to do.

Point of Truth: You and I can love Jesus enough to love and forgive anyone He can love.

God says in 1 John 2:9 **He that saith he is in the light, and hateth his brother, is in darkness even until now. 10 He that loveth his brother abideth in the light, and there is none occasion of stumbling in him.** The Greek word for "**stumbling**" carries the idea of *a trap, a snare*. When you love others, as an obedient believer, you are abiding in the light, thus you can see and avoid the traps the enemy sets for you as he attempts to ensnare you.

1. Is there anyone you do not want to love and forgive because of a past offense? _____
2. Is there anyone you do not want to love because of his/her race? _____
3. Is there anyone you are not willing to love because he/she holds different doctrinal or political opinions than you? _____ Loving and forgiving others does not imply that you approve of their behavior or agree with their ideas. God loves us even when we are wrong. His love for us never changes. It is unconditional.
4. Read the following:

A YOUNG MAN AND HIS JOURNEY

To illustrate what it means to do all things "**heartily as unto the Lord, and not unto men,**" I share this story which has helped me communicate this principle. A few years ago I shared a message from Colossians 3:23 **And**

whatsoever ye do, do it heartily, as to the Lord, and not unto men.

I challenged everyone to not do one thing tomorrow unless they did it as unto the Lord. I challenged homemakers to do their housework for Jesus and not the family alone. I challenged workers to do their jobs for Jesus. I challenged young people in school to go to class and do their work just for Jesus. I challenged them to write Col. 3:23 on index cards and place them where they would see them throughout the day as a reminder of who they are really living and working for.

The next night a fourteen-year-old boy came to me. He told how his grandfather had bought some beagle dogs so they could hunt rabbits. Upon the purchase of the dogs they made an agreement. He said, "The agreement was Grandpa would buy the dogs and feed. My job would be to feed them each day and keep the pens clean." He told how at first the chores were no problem because he likes to hunt rabbits. But after hunting season, he grew tired of tending to them and especially cleaning the pens.

As he spoke, he became excited. He said, "I listened to what you said last night about doing everything we are supposed to do just for Jesus and not because we have to do it. I got up this morning before school and fed the dogs without having to be told. When I came home from school, I cleaned the pens without being told." He said, "I can't remember feeding the dogs and cleaning the pen without being threatened with discipline. But today I fed them and cleaned those pens just for Jesus."

He became more excited and said, "It wasn't nearly as hard as it was when I did it because I had to. And, I cleaned the pens better than I had before. It is true; when you do your work just for Jesus you can even enjoy doing a good job."

I said, "Young man, if you will treasure Jesus enough to do your responsibilities for Him, He will be pleased to fulfill His will for your life through you." I told him how employers are looking for people who are driven to do a good job and there is no better reason for wanting to do all things well than knowing Jesus will be pleased. God will open greater doors of opportunity for all who treasure Jesus by striving to do His will.

The same results have been reported by many others concerning their regular responsibilities. This one verse (Col. 3:23) has enough life changing power to transform any believer's life. If you find yourself frustrated and/or resentful as you do your responsibilities, how about striving to do all you do just for Jesus. Write out Colossians 3:23 and put it where you will see it as you do your daily responsibilities. So the way to "Keep Your Heart on God" is to do everything you do "**heartily**" as unto Jesus, and not unto men. The word heartily speaks of passion, desire and love.

Desperation and desire for God are two essential keys to having personal revival. What will it take to produce these in us?

"The primary qualification for a missionary is not love for souls, as we often hear, but love for Christ."

--Vance Havner, Endnote 9

Week Four, Day One
Where Jesus Leads, I Will Walk with Him with All of My Heart.
Defeating Temptation Takes Place in Your Mind.

 Memory verse– Eph. 6:7 **With good will doing service, as to the Lord, and not to men:**

Today, we will examine God's instructions in Hebrews 12:1-4 for defeating temptation.

1 Wherefore seeing we also are compassed about with so great a cloud of witnesses, let us lay aside every weight, and the sin which doth so easily beset us, and let us run with patience the race that is set before us,

Everyone who has conquered a temptation or a stronghold is a witness of the power of Christ to change a person's life and make him/her free. There are millions of witnesses to the fact that Jesus can and will make believers free from dominating sins so each one is free to love and live victoriously in Him.

Is your goal for freedom so you can abide in loving fellowship with Jesus? _____ Or, is your motive merely self-centered so you can live your life devoted to something else, namely yourself? God makes us free when our hearts are about Jesus. Make sure your goal is a closer walk with Him, which results in a joyous life in Him (See John 15:11). The freedom and peace you want can only be found in love-driven desire for Jesus.

Because we are believers, we are being watched by others. This is another reason we need to strive to be faithful in every way we can. It is important for all who claim to be Jesus' followers to live like it. <u>You are a witness</u> for Him. You are either a good witness or a bad one.

Your mind is the main spiritual battleground of your life. Spiritual battles take place in our minds. Our minds are directly and powerfully influenced by our hearts (our desires, loves and affections). To run the race of faith as Jesus commands, you must first win the battle against wrong in your mind. The main weapon against sin is God's Word, Truth. You must learn and accept truth while rejecting every false way of thinking.

The verse above says there are two things that God expects us to do to run our races effectively. First, we are to **lay aside every weight**. The idea of **weight** to a runner is anything that can be laid aside so he/she doesn't carry an unnecessary hindrance. **Every weight** can mean good or bad things. Sometimes believers come to see their hearts are entangled with too many **weights**, too many good things, to effectively treasure Jesus as they should. So, they must identify and confront the things that hinder them from loving Jesus as they should.

Secondly, we are to lay aside **the sin,** wrong things, which hinder successful, fruitful running in loving fellowship with Jesus. This one is self-explanatory. We know sins are wrong. We know they hinder us as we strive to walk with Jesus in love. The worse thing about sin is the separating it does to close fellowship with Jesus.

Your heart can be given to both good things and bad things. Whatever has your heart, has you. It is controlling you. It is greatly impacting your life. It is the magnet that has the major pull on your life. As God sees things, whatever has your heart has control of your life.

How do we lay those weights and sins aside when temptation can be so powerful? By 2 **<u>Looking unto Jesus</u> the author and finisher of our faith;**

who for the joy that was set before him endured the cross, despising the shame, and is set down at the right hand of the throne of God. So, what does **looking unto Jesus** mean? It means to focus intently upon Him through the eyes of your mind. To think about Him and His love for you. You are to confront temptation with a long and intensive look at Jesus by thinking about Him. So when you are tempted, think about Jesus, desire Him, treasure Him more than all else by believing He loves and cares for you. This is the life that leads to victory.

Jesus is the "**author and finisher of our faith**;" The idea of the word **author** is actually, *leader, captain, guide and protector.* **Looking unto Jesus** is exactly the same as looking to truth, because they are the same. When tempted, fill your mind with Jesus, truth about Him and yourself in Him. Envision Him taking your death, so you can live with Him in loving intimacy now and forever. Picture yourself as His bride, robed in pure righteousness, thus without spot, wrinkle or any other blemish. Imagine you, standing with Jesus and you are shining in the brightness of His glory.

To look to Jesus as we should, we are told, 3 **For consider him that endured such contradiction of sinners against himself, lest ye be wearied and faint in your minds.** What happens to believers who fail to look to Jesus, to **consider him**, when tempted? They become **wearied and faint** in their **minds**, thus, they lose the battle and stop running faithfully and effectively. What are you to **consider** when focusing on Jesus? You must **consider him that endured such contradiction of sinners against himself.** Think about Him and His suffering for you, so He can have you as His own. When you are tempted to sin, picture Jesus in His suffering and death for you personally. Think about what dying for you cost Him as He paid your sin debts. Think about what He paid to enable you can refuse temptation and no longer serve sin. Think about how He revealed His love for you when He died in your place, under your condemnation, your judgment. Think about how much God loves you to have given His Son to die in your place. 1 John 4:19 **We love him, because he first loved us.** If you don't know and believe (accept fully) how deeply God loves you, then you will not be enabled to love Him. Your love for God flows out of knowing, accepting, receiving, and believing that He really does love you unconditionally so He can have you for Himself.

It is difficult to continue in temptation when you are focusing on Jesus' suffering and death so He can have you for Himself. It is as though you must step over or tread upon Him, His love, His sacrifice of Himself, to commit that sin. Thinking of Jesus suffering in your place to make you free to be His in every way causes you to be mindful of how horrible your sins actually are and how damaging they are to love-driven companionship with Him. If the eyes of your mind are on the Captain of your faith, you will win.

Here is one thing you can be sure of, refusing to sin will not kill you. Don't believe the lie that it will. 4 **Ye have not yet resisted unto blood, striving against sin.** This verse lets us know this passage is teaching how to win **against sin**, how to defeat temptation. You don't have it as bad as Jesus did. Consider this: If you are reading this, then you are alive, therefore, your striving to be faithful has not been as hard on you as it was Jesus.

Thinking of Jesus, **looking** to Him, **consider**ing Him, is turning to Him for help and refuge. God says in James 4:8 **Draw nigh to God, and he will draw nigh to you. . . .**

When you treasure Jesus as you should, it will be in your heart to do what is right. God says be faithful and win in your mind by **looking unto Jesus the author and finisher of our faith. Point of Truth: When you treasure Jesus more than what you get from your sin, you win.**

Temptation works through your mind. When you are tempted, you begin to picture in your mind what that sin can give to you. If you focus on the sin, you become weaker and weaker in your resolve to refuse it. Don't think about the short-term gratification that sin gives. When temptation comes, train yourself to treasure Jesus while thinking of His suffering for you to make you free to express your love to Him through obedience.

Jesus died for us to destroy the "**body of sin**", therefore we should no longer **serve sin.** Romans 6:6 **Knowing this, that our old man is crucified with** *him,* **that the body of sin might be destroyed, that henceforth we should not serve sin.** The idea of **body of sin** points to the fact of an influence that exists in our lives that wants us to give in to temptations. Temptation is like a former slave master who will not let go, even though the slave has been legally and rightfully freed. Jesus is the new Master who freed us from the rights of our old sin master. We no longer have to serve sins and **should not**. When temptation asks for your attention, give your attention more intently to Jesus. Show the devil that anytime he tempts you to sin, you are going to think about Jesus and what He paid so you can say "no" to sin. The devil will soon see that tempting you is counterproductive to his cause, because it drives you to Jesus, to appreciating and loving Him more by thinking of how He gave Himself up for you so you can give yourself up for Him.

When you look to Jesus as you strive against sin, you can rightfully see He paid everything needed to empower you to live free from sin's dominion. In Jesus, you also see you can win over temptation because He loves you and has a high purpose for your obedience. A good, long consideration of Jesus energizes your soul. It empowers you as you draw upon His strength.

If you don't believe Jesus' death did enough to make you free, then you are saying His death is not enough, thus God giving His Son to die for you is insufficient. That is a horrible rebuke to God. Seeing God did give His Son to save you, you must know He will give you the freedom you need to walk with Him. Romans 8:32 **He that spared not his own Son, but delivered him up for us all, how shall he not with him also freely give us all things?** With Jesus comes all we need to be the persons He desires.

The battle against sin is won or lost in your mind and heart. If you win in your thought life and affections, you win in your actions. If you lose in your thought life, you will lose in your actions.

1. Has God shown to you a "good" thing, a "**weight**" that you need to lay aside so you can run your race of faith more effectively? _____ If so, list it here: _____

2. Has God shown you a sin/s that you must turn from? _____ If so, make a strong and firm surrender to Jesus by treasuring Him so much that you take brutal action against that sin. Treat and look upon that sin like the hostile, destructive enemy it is. Sin is a spiritual terrorist that wants to destroy you, so treat it that way.

Week Four, Day Two
Where Jesus Leads, I Will Walk with Him with All of My Heart.
Walking Joyfully with Jesus.

 Memory verse– Eph. 6:7 **With good will doing service, as to the Lord, and not to men.**

As you set your heart on Jesus, you are step-by-step made free to live in stride with Him and His will. As your heart remains fixed on Jesus, there is no longer a personal agenda ruling your life. Your desires and ambitions are absorbed into your desire to please Him, therefore you voluntarily submit to His will. Whatever God removes from your life and plans must be considered sacrifices to Him. Whatever He lets you retain of your personal desires and goals must be considered privileges. All of life is to be hidden (concealed and lived) in Christ. Colossians 3:1 **If ye then be risen with Christ, seek those things which are above, where Christ sitteth on the right hand of God. 2 Set your affection** (heart of love) **on things <u>above</u>, not on things on the earth. 3 For ye are <u>dead</u>, and your life is hid with <u>Christ</u> in God. 4 When Christ, who is <u>our</u> life, shall appear, then shall ye also appear with him in glory.** God is all about LIFE and GLORY. We live by His life and shine by His glory. He put His life and glory in us to display His glory, especially the glory of His Son.

Who is "**our life**?" _____ Have you realized Jesus is your life? _____ There is no other productive way to live than to live with your heart of love after Him. Any other approach to life is empty and disappointing.

Do you realize that you are on this earth for God Himself, to display His glory? _____

I have been asked, "Isn't this joyful life a place of maturity that we all are to grow into?" I answered "I don't think so." Have you noticed often when a person is first saved how he/she is filled with joy? Sometimes older Christians will look at a new convert and think he/she is certainly confused and possibly not truly saved. They come to this conclusion because the old, worldly way of life is often very visible in new believers.

New believers may not know the "church language" at first. They tend to use terms from the old life when they speak about God, and they may dress and wear styles like their culture. I can imagine a teenager with a multicolored hair style being saved and giving testimony the following Sunday in the average church. There would be people who could not believe what they were hearing. Some would never hear the new convert's message because of his/her appearance. Yet, that new convert might be more joyful in Jesus than they are.

I'll explain. When a person gets saved, he/she is saved by receiving Jesus Christ as his/her Lord and Savior. When a person receives Jesus (which happens by believing God has raised Him from the dead and confessing Him as Lord), God saves that person the same way He saves others. His joy floods his/her heart, because the new believer's heart has turned to Him. This joy is flowing from Jesus. John 15:11 **These things have I spoken unto <u>you</u>, that <u>my</u> joy might remain in you, and that your joy might be <u>full</u>.** The problem for many is Jesus' joy does not **remain** as it should because their hearts are not kept on Him, which is revealed in many ways. Such as, failing to trust Him. Or, being satisfied with where they are spiritually. Or, treasuring things of this world, thus, trying to serve two gods.

Biblical joy is not something you grow to someday obtain. The joy of Jesus is where His life is flowing through you in unhindered ways.

What causes someone to lose joy? Joy is lost when the heart, or part of it, shifts away from the Jesus. When your heart departs from Jesus, whether in part or in whole, the joy of Jesus no longer flows freely through you. Jesus is still there and His Word still has influence on you, but the joy is hindered, thus not **full**. However, your gifts continue to operate, and this has caused a lot of confusion.

Even when your heart is treasuring something other than Jesus, others may still be blessed by your gifts, talents or ministries. People may get saved when you preach, give your testimony, or witness to them. Even when your heart is not right, God's Word is still powerful in touching hearts and lives when it is shared. And, God tells how the gifts bestowed upon a believer will remain active in him/her no matter what the person does. Romans 11:29 **For the gifts and calling of God are without repentance.** Many translate "**without repentance**" as "irrevocable" meaning *they cannot be changed or taken away*. God does this to show He is committed to bringing to completion the work He started in us because we have been redeemed by His Son, through His suffering and death, for the purpose of His Son's glory.

When your heart is fixed on Jesus, a more powerful working of His Spirit flows through you, and people are blessed and touched more deeply. It is not you, but Christ in you touching the world as your gifts function. Just because your gifts bless others does not mean you are walking closely with Jesus. So, a believer should never use his/her "effectiveness" in Christian service to justify his/her sins or lack of obedience in Christian disciplines and responsibilities, thus his/her lack of walking with Jesus in love. Spiritual gifts continue to function to some degree because they are irrevocable.

Point of Truth: Just because there are spiritual results does not mean the best is being done.

Some believers and churches make compromises in attempts to grow. There is no need to compromise God's Word. What is needed is for the people of God to come back to Jesus with all of our hearts. When we do return to Him, we find there is no need to compromise. Be sure to know God is not against change as long as the change does not compromise Scripture. Many believers and churches miss God's best because they refuse to change their methods of ministry and outreach. God uses different methods, but He <u>**never**</u> leads His people to violate His Word. We should use methods of ministry that best relate to those we are seeking to minister to or reach with the gospel, and many times that requires change in our methods.

What happened to Christians who have lost Christ's joy? Their hearts have departed from Him in part or in whole. Those who shift away from Him in part may remain faithful to the church and His work but have no consistent joy. Those who depart completely may have never been genuinely saved, so they usually drop away from Him and His people as explained in 1 John 2:19 **They went out from us, but they were not of us; for if they had been of us, they would *no doubt* have continued with us: but *they went out,* that they might be made manifest that they were not all of us.** When people depart, we know other things have their hearts, or they possibly were never truly saved. While those remaining in Jesus' work without His joy are puzzling. It is likely their hearts have shifted to serving the ministry, themselves, the power associated with a position, or something else.

1. Write this week's memory verse. _____

Write the most insightful thing you are learning in this study. _____

3. Pray for your pastor, church staff, deacons and other church leaders.
Jeremiah 29:13 **And <u>ye</u> shall <u>seek</u> me, and <u>find</u> me, when ye shall <u>search</u> for me with all your <u>heart</u>.**
The words "**seek**" "**find**" and "**search**" portray the idea of mining for gold, silver or another treasure. There is diligence and exciting expectations infused in them. Jesus wants you to seek Him as you would seek for the greatest thing you might treasure.

As the Apostle Paul pled with God to remove one severe problem in his life, God told him that He had a purpose for not removing that problem and He would give him grace to endure it. God also told him that his problem would be a greater platform for usefulness and effectiveness in life and ministry, so Paul chose to glory in ALL of his problems.

When Paul didn't get what he asked for, read what God said to him in 2 Corinthians 12:9-10 (in the box). It may seem odd to think of the Apostle Paul living daily with the strong sense of his weaknesses, but he did. He continually lived under the strain and stress of the things I have underlined in this passage. Like us, he lived with feelings that he had to reject by faith day by day, but he also lived with feelings of weaknesses and pressures that he understood were his platform of greater usefulness in Christ's kingdom. A person can't go through the things listed in this passage and always feel as though he/she is on top of the world. Don't be surprised when your weaknesses cause you to feel weak in yourself, thus under pressure, which is designed to drive you to greater dependence on Jesus and less on yourself. (See 2 Cor. 1:9). When you feel weak in yourself, you are less dependent on yourself and less prideful over your strengths and accomplishments.

If Paul had gotten what he asked for (relief from his problem) he wouldn't have sensed the need for God's grace as he did. It is the same for you, when things go as you want, you don't sense your need for God and His grace to get you through in victory. However, when you do not get what you want in life, you can glory in His grace as you endure living with your weaknesses, thus the infirmities of your life and mind that you can't change.

The feelings of inadequacy and weakness that come with life on earth in our physical bodies and minds are there to drive us to dependence on Jesus. Yes, ask for your problems to be removed and if God does, praise Him for it, but if He doesn't, don't belittle and degrade yourself. Don't look upon your weaknesses as rejection by God or a lack of His love for you. Look upon them as they really are, a place to demonstrate and express faith in Him. Use your weaknesses to stand strong in His grace, in spite of how you feel, and He will reveal His life and power in and through you. When you trust Jesus, in spite of your circumstances and how you feel, you can expect God to do greater things in and through you because you are depending on Him.

At times, our feelings are not aligned with truth. Feelings can lie to you. They can make you think things that are not accurate about yourself, others, and God. What God says is true, and He says **IF** you will depend on Him, you can learn to glory in your weaknesses, adversities and trials. Which transforms them into platforms of pleasure because they serve to release God's power in your life. When you feel inadequate for all God wants you to be and do, you can and should trust only in Him, thus less in yourself. (Read the illustration in the box).

> 2 Corinthians 12:9 **And he said unto me, My grace is sufficient for thee: for my strength is made perfect in weakness. Most gladly therefore will I rather glory in <u>my infirmities</u>, that the power of Christ may rest upon me. 10 Therefore I take pleasure <u>in infirmities, in reproaches, in necessities, in persecutions, in distresses</u> for Christ's sake: for when I am weak, then am I strong.**

> Suppose I am about to preach a sermon. I have prepared and studied well, but I still feel very inadequate to effectively deliver the message. So, I cry out to God in my weakness. As long as I prepare and preach, fully aware of my inabilities, I depend on His Spirit as fully as I can. In that condition of heart and action, God's power can be displayed in me. My weaknesses serve to keep me humbly aware of my need for God. It is the same for all areas of our lives. When we think we can handle life, we don't depend on God as we should, therefore we don't see His power displayed in us as it could have been. How much do you depend on God?

Week Four, Day Three
Where Jesus Leads, I Will Walk with Him with All of My Heart.
Revival and Your Walk with Jesus.

 Memory verse- Eph. 6:7 **With good will doing service, as to the Lord, and not to men:**

Today you will read about your spiritual journey. The moment you were saved, the Lord Jesus came into your life to dwell, and that changed everything. Knowing He lives in every believer, then why doesn't He flow His joy through each one as He would like? Because many hearts are not kept on Him. This may have happened because they didn't know to serve Him in love, but rather, sought to do His will out of a sense of duty and obligation.

You are on a spiritual journey with Jesus where He wants you to walk closely with Him in a love-driven relationship. He saved you for Himself. You are always on your spiritual journey, and everything you are responsible to be and do is part of your spiritual journey to maturity in Him.

Some have mistakenly divided their lives into segments. Sundays are given to participating in spiritual things, but on Monday they feel they are doing secular things. That is not the case. From God's perspective, everything a believer does is holy and should be done for Jesus.

Your life and work are just as important to God as anyone's because He is at work in you in all things to display His Son's glory. You might be operating a machine at work. If you run that machine "**heartily, as unto the Lord, and not unto men**" you have kept your heart on Him, even though your thoughts were intent upon that work. You might be washing clothes, cooking, or cleaning your house, or you may be serving in the nursery at church, etc. Whatever you do, learn to do all for Jesus' sake, to be pleasing to Him, and then your work is just as honorable and holy as anyone's.

Do your responsibilities as though Jesus were there with you, because He is. He is watching you to see why and how diligently you do the things you are responsible to do.

Point of Truth: It's not the place you work that makes your work spiritually significant, but rather the person to whom your labor is done.

Think of your daily life with Jesus as "Your Journey in Spiritual Growth." Notice in the following verses how the word **walk** refers to a believer's daily life with Jesus. Romans 8:1 **There is therefore now no condemnation to them which are in Christ Jesus, who walk not after the flesh, but after the Spirit.** And, Colossians 1:10 **That ye might walk worthy of the Lord unto all pleasing, being fruitful in every good work, and increasing in the knowledge of God.** And, 1 John 2:6 **He that saith he abideth in him** (Jesus) **ought himself also to walk, even as he walked.**

Your journey with Jesus is filled with mountain tops and valleys. Everyone travels a road mixed with good and hard times. When sin came into the world, this earth was cursed with troubles and death. Because of sin, everyone suffers from time to time. No one lives without troubles. No one is exempt from the ups and downs of life.

You have a heart which can be controlled by your own will and desires. You can walk through life knowing how to immediately return to Jesus when you discover you have departed. You can walk with Jesus moment by moment if you will. I am not saying you will live sinlessly perfect. But I am saying you can have the will to do so and you can strive to do so.

Some might ask "Doesn't a lost person travel the same road of life?" Everyone travels a road filled with ups and downs. The lost person is led by the **world** (a system that opposes God and His will), the **flesh** (the worldly desires and appetites of fallen man), and the **devil** (Satan and his evil forces). The following passage shows how these are the ones the unsaved walk with, even though they may not be aware of it. Eph. 2:1 **And you hath he quickened, who were dead in trespasses and sins: 2 Wherein in time past ye <u>walked</u>** (were led by and lived with) **according to the course of this world, according to the prince of the power of the air, the spirit that now worketh in the children of disobedience: 3 Among whom also we all had our <u>conversation</u> in times past in the lusts of our flesh, fulfilling the desires of the flesh and of the mind; and were by nature the children of wrath, even as others.** According to verse one, what was your condition before you were saved? "**dead in _____**"

The human race was produced through Adam and Eve, who died spiritually from innocence when they sinned the first time (Rom. 5:12). Therefore every unsaved person is dead (separated) spiritually toward God because his/her death came by sin. Everyone has a sinful nature as Adam did. Everyone is separated spiritually from God, until each one is saved. As soon as a person receives Jesus Christ as Lord and Savior, he/she is made spiritually alive toward God because Jesus is now in him/her.

The word "**conversation**" is sometimes translated *behave* (1 Tim. 3:15), *behavior, or lifestyle*. These verses tell how a lost person is being led by forces that oppose God. Unsaved people think they are calling the shots in their lives. They feel they are in control of their lives when they are not. God says they are led through life by "**the world, the flesh, and the devil**. That is why unsaved persons easily distance themselves from God. The "god" they are walking with works to make them think they are okay spiritually. The **world, the flesh, and the devil** work to blind them to their need of Jesus as Lord and Savior. The devil uses anything he can to convince the unsaved that they do not need Jesus as their Lord and Savior. For unsaved persons in bondage (addicted to a particular sin) he uses that sin to keep them from wanting Jesus. For the morally "good," he uses their own good works (their self-righteousness) to cause them think they are acceptable to God in and of themselves.

Point of Truth: The devil doesn't have to make a guy uncommonly evil to keep him unsaved. All he has to do is keep him blinded to the truth of God's love for him, thus his need of Jesus.

Anyone without Christ is lost, dead spiritually toward God in sin, just as the most ungodly are lost. There is no difference in "lostness" between the so called "good" and the "bad." Everyone without Christ is separated spiritually from God. One may be more obviously a sinner in the eyes of others, but God sees all without Jesus as ungodly and evil. Actually, the most sinful will more readily see his/her sinful condition and admit it. While the "good" person compares himself/herself to others and thinks God is pleased with his/her self-righteousness. Yet, without the cleansing blood of Jesus (which is applied to the new believer the moment Christ is received), the best person is dead in sin even if he/she is active in church work.

Being dead in sins does not mean the unsaved person is not a spiritual being and has not possibly had spiritual experiences. Satan and his workers can appear as spiritual beings of light. (See 2 Corinthians 11:14). Therefore, an unsaved person can have "spiritual" experiences that are not of God.

When a believer departs from Jesus in his/her heart, at that point, he/she is also greatly influenced by the world, the flesh, and the devil. Such believers have a heart problem, a love problem.

Just because you are saved does not mean you are free from the influence of these three. You are always subject to being influenced by the powers around you. When Jesus' life is flowing through you, these enemies have no control (no dominating influence) over you. When you draw near to Jesus with all of your heart, the devil will flee from you, the flesh will increasingly be made to submit to the new man in you (that part of you that is indwelt by the Holy Spirit). The world will lose its alluring influence over you because you are treasuring Jesus, loving Him, and He is so much more than they have to offer. If you treasure Jesus as you should, you will strive to keep your heart toward Him, and you will recognize when you heart is being drawn away after inferior things.

1. Are you consciously striving to walk closely with Jesus in a love-driven relationship? _____ If so, how? _____

2. Have you purposed in your heart to walk with Jesus no matter the costs? _____

3. Seek the face of God. Nothing is better than being face-to-face with your most intimate friend.

In the previous lesson, you read about your weaknesses and how they can keep you from living a life of significance. The first, normal reaction to negative things in your life that you can't change is to want to hide them or run away from them. As you grow closer to Jesus, you realize your weakness are there to help you forsake self-dependence so you will rely on Jesus every moment or every day.

Everything changes in Jesus. Even the worst things can be transformed into things that make you spiritually strong in Him. God has a High Purpose for everything, even the things we can't understand. We can trust Him and triumph in Him, in all things, if we will to do so.

Point of Truth: Every believer is only a few decisions away from Personal Revival.

When you choose to embrace life in Jesus to the point that you believe He is working all things together for your, ultimate good, your faith places you in the position for your heart to turn more fully to Him. When your heart is turned to Him as fully as it can be, personal revival happens. It happens in Jesus, because He is life. He is revival.

If you are not using your weaknesses as platforms for drawing closer to Jesus, (which causes a person to find significance in life) what do you suppose would happen if you began to do so now and from this day forward?

_____

Week Four, Day Four
Where Jesus Leads, I Will Walk with Him with All of My Heart.
Walking with Jesus in Obedience for His Glory.

 Memory verse- Eph. 6:7 **With good will doing service, as to the Lord, and not to men:**

When God finds a believer striving to walk closely with Jesus, therefore, willing to trust Him, no matter the cost, He shows His mighty power through that person. 2 Chronicles 16:9 **For the eyes of the LORD run to and fro throughout the whole earth, to show himself strong in the behalf of them whose heart is** <u>perfect</u> **toward him. . . .**

The word "**perfect**" means *completely*
-Strong's Hebrew Dictionary H8003.

God is looking at you to see if He will find a "**whole**" (complete) heart toward Him, so He can **show Himself strong** on your **behalf**.

Jesus wants you, not something you can give to Him apart from yourself. Acts 17:24 **God that made the world and all things therein, seeing that he is Lord of heaven and earth, dwelleth not in temples made with hands;** 25 **Neither is worshiped with men's hands, as though he needed any thing, seeing he giveth to all life, and breath, and all things;** God created and owns everything; how could He need anything from anyone? He doesn't have needs, but He does have desires. He desires to have your heart, so He can share life with you moment by moment, whereby His Son is revealed in you as the Great God and Savior that He is. God is working in you to show how effective His Son is in saving and transforming each one's life from a heart purposed toward other things, to a heart driven by love for Him and His will. God has purposed to exalt Jesus, and Jesus has purposed to exalt His Father. Some very good news is they have included you in a huge aspect of fulfilling these purposes. God's highest purpose is His glory and He has included you in revealing His glory in this world and the world to come.

A common error is to think if you correct your lifestyle, God will be pleased with you and, therefore, personal revival will be yours. Correcting your lifestyle while Jesus does not have your heart leads to disillusionment and confusion. It is common that once a believer corrects his/her lifestyle, he/she expects a victorious spiritual life. Such incorrect thinking can lead to a wrecked faith. It can open one to false teachings and the cults of this world, and at the very least, self-pity and discouragement.

Point of Truth: A correct heart results in walking closely with Jesus, out of which flows a desire and striving for obedience so He will be exalted in you.

God's work in us is being accomplished to bring each one to a heart fixed on Jesus, so the Holy Spirit will metamorphically change each one into His moral image. The Christian life is much more than what you do. It is what you are becoming with Jesus flowing His life in and through you so freely that you give up your life to Him. Galatians 2:20 **I am crucified <u>with</u> Christ: nevertheless I live; yet not <u>I</u>, but <u>Christ</u> liveth in <u>me</u>: and the life which I <u>now</u> <u>live</u> in the flesh I live by the <u>faith</u> of the Son of God, who <u>loved</u> me, and <u>gave</u> <u>himself</u> for me.** Did Jesus give something or Himself so He could have you as His own? _____ He wants you to give yourself to Him in return.

In the mind of God, every member of Jesus' body was taken to the cross crucified with Him, so He not only died for us, we died with Him. When He was baptized into death, so were we. We also were resurrected in Him and have His resurrected life in us.

Romans 6:6 **Knowing this, that our old man is crucified with him, that the body of sin might be destroyed, that henceforth we should not serve sin.** Jesus included us in His death to destroy the "**body of sin**" thus, the controlling mastery of sin so we can serve Him. He destroyed the "**body of sin**" in such a way **"that henceforth we should not serve sin"** therefore, we are not obligated to obey sin's commands. Sin is no longer our master.

When a slave dies, he is freed from slavery. We should see ourselves freed from sin's dominion because when Jesus died, we died with Him. When He rose from the dead, He raised us up too. He included us in His death and resurrection to break sin's dominance over us. Therefore, every believer has died to his/her old sin master. Therefore, in Jesus, we can enjoy life together with Him now and Him forever. (See Romans 6). He saved us for Himself.

Sin should not be a master to believers. A master tells his slave what to do, therefore, a slave serves his master. Because Jesus included you in His death, you no longer have to walk with and serve your old sin master. You are free to walk with Jesus and serve Him with all of your heart. If you treasure Jesus enough, you will strive to not allow sin to have its way with you.

Sin will offer you things it thinks you want, hoping you will treasure those things more than you treasure Jesus. That is how temptation works. It works through your heart, your desires. Temptation has no power in your life except where you have a desire for something it has to offer. So, your desires lead to your sins. However, your desires can be changed by knowing HOW deeply Jesus loves you. He changes your desires by transforming you into His own likeness.

There are at least four options you may take in response to His love and call to obedience.

1. You may resist because you feel inadequate. You don't think you are prepared and fitted for the place of ministry to which you are being called.
2. You may refuse because you don't want to do it. This is when God's plan doesn't fit into your plan for your life.
3. You may resist because you do not have enough faith in God or yourself (that God will do it through you or you are afraid you will not follow through). You are simply weak in faith.
4. You trust and follow Jesus in love, no matter the costs.

As you journey through each day with Jesus, He will occasionally lead you to stumbling blocks, "points of turning." You must repent if the stumbling block is a sin, or follow by faith if the stumbling block is a call to service/ministry. Stumbling blocks (resistance to obey a call to Christian service or resistance to repent of a sin) are usually pointed out to you when you are in a valley (a difficult time in life).

In a down time of life (a time of trouble and adversity), you are more likely to be open to instruction from Jesus. When things seem to fall apart in your life, you are more aware of your need to be changed. When you suffer, you more readily become discontented with the way you are. When you are hurting, you can better see how useless it is to attempt to live without being right with Jesus in every way.

As you travel through life, you will have ups and downs, even if your heart is fixed on Jesus. But, some of the things Jesus might take you through you could avoid if you would judge yourself and turn to Him as best as you can. Trusting God does not mean every obedience leads to a comfortable and convenient place in life. Sometimes we must suffer for doing what is right which ultimately leads to a better place.

As you study God's Word with your heart fixed on Jesus, He will reveal the hidden things of your life, the things that need to be changed.

Point of Truth: Many believers are not ready to deal with the hidden things because they have not turned from the sins they know about.

If you refuse to turn from sin or anything else that has your heart, your fellowship with Jesus will be interrupted. At that point, a stumbling block is between you and Jesus, and the gap between where you are spiritually and where He wants you grows wider.

1. Is Jesus calling you to surrender and devote yourself to a place in ministry? _____
2. As a pattern, when has God spoken to you more clearly- in an "up time" or a "down time" of life? _____
3. In obedience to God's Word, pray for your government leaders (1 Timothy 2:1-3).
4. Pray for our police, firefighters, emergency care personnel and military personnel.
6. Pray for missionaries who are spreading the gospel around the world.

Week Four, Day Five
Where Jesus Leads, I Will Walk with Him with All of My Heart.
What is in Your Eye?

 Memory verse– Eph. 6:7 **With good will doing service, as to the Lord, and not to men:**

God wants a better future for His children. To have the future He wants for you, you must take some deliberate and intentional steps of obedience based only on love for Jesus. One key is learning His Word and applying the insights gained to your everyday life. The following passage speaks to your life and the things He has entrusted to you. Matthew 6:19 **Lay not up for yourselves treasures upon earth, where moth and rust doth corrupt, and where thieves break through and steal: 20 But lay up for yourselves treasures in heaven, where neither moth nor rust doth corrupt, and where thieves do not break through nor steal: 21 For where your treasure is, there will your heart be also.**

Jesus' plan for our treasures is quite different than we might naturally think. His plan calls for a future that goes beyond this life. The dividends from His plan last longer and achieve higher goals.

Jesus is not saying you should not wisely plan for tomorrow on earth. Much of the Bible's teaching on stewardship is about being prepared to do God's work today and until He calls us home. What Jesus confronts is the attitude that causes a person to hoard things, without considering a greater investment for wealth.

God's focus in this passage is on unused or misused treasures. Unused, hoarded treasures make no positive impact in anyone's life. Actually, they are only making an impact on the lives of those who hoard them, but the impact is negative. And, the misuse of treasures doesn't work in the purposes of God. Misused treasures can actually work against God and His purposes by drawing one's heart toward things that will not endure eternally.

Hoarded treasures may possibly draw your heart away from God, just like overly desiring treasures you do not have. There is no difference in the outcome. One person has money and treasures it above God. Another wants more money so much that God is not in his/her focus. Both end in the same place, God and His purposes are neglected.

Jesus, speaking along this same line, said in Luke 12:33 **Sell that ye have, and give alms; provide yourselves bags which wax not old, a treasure in the heavens that faileth not, where no thief approacheth, neither moth corrupteth. 34 For where your treasure is, there will your heart be also.** What Jesus was expressing might practically be stated, "Do you own your possessions or do they own you?" So, to test yourself, you can consider the thought of "giving all of your treasures away to help those who are hurting." How does this thought strike you? _____
_____ Such thoughts help us assess the connection we have with our possessions.

The statement "**For where your treasure is, there will your heart be also**" is what I call "a principle statement." It is a statement that centers on the main point of a passage. It is a statement that does not change in context or out. Biblical principles like this one are clear and unchanging. So, whatever you choose to "**treasure**" will soon have your heart.

Verse 33 is not necessarily a command that every believer is expected to do. Many of the most influential persons in the Bible owned things and managed them well for God's glory. Verse 33 is something to consider, so you can assess where your heart really is. (Although, God may speak to anyone's heart at any given time to give everything away and follow Him, and many have in obedience to His call).

Matthew 6:19-20 sets up verse 21 **For where your treasure is, there will your heart be also.** Verses 19 & 20 appeal to us on the grounds of the reasonableness that treasures stored on earth deteriorate in comparison to treasures stored in heaven. Stored treasures have no eternal value. However, they can have by being used for the advancement Jesus' kingdom. And that is where verse 20 comes in. 20 **But lay up for yourselves treasures in heaven, where neither moth nor rust doth corrupt, and where thieves do not break through nor steal:**

Then, Jesus gives deeper insight in Matthew 6:22 **The light of the body is the eye: if therefore thine eye be single, thy whole body shall be full of light.** The word "**single**" is interesting and yet seams somewhat obscure. It was translated from two Greek words. The basic meaning is *"folded together."* So, you could read the statement of verse 22 as, "**The light of the body is the eye: if therefore thine eye be** *folded together***, thy whole body shall be full of light.**"

Jesus was striving to get His listeners to be sure they were not attempting to serve two gods, namely God and money, as verse 24 states. To do this, Jesus taught the way to avoid making the tragic mistake of trying to serve God and money is to make sure your eye, the vision of your life and mind, is *folded* into one thing.

In other words, your life does consist of many important things, and rightfully so. Yet, there is a way to bring all of your life into a "**single**" unit and that by making everything about Jesus and His glory.

When you consider the word Jesus used, it makes perfect sense to those who are striving to be His in every way. When our lives have one, **single**, purpose in view (Jesus) for doing all we do and for all we have, we are at our best.

God makes your life fruitful in many ways for the glory of Jesus. Such as talents, gifts, skills and possessions. These are for you to hold up before the world for His glory. Jesus taught in John 15 that He flows His life through His followers to produce spiritual fruit in us so we can **bear** (hold up) that fruit to glorify His Father.

Point of Truth: The Father is about glorifying His Son, and Jesus is about glorifying His Father. God exists in His glory and does all things to display His glory.

We "hold up" all we are and have by flowing everything back to Jesus thus, treasuring Him for His glory.

So, a **single** eye has one **treasure** in focus. That does not mean there are not other things in your life. It means everything in your life is to focus on Jesus. We are to treasure Him with all of our hearts. You see when your eye is focused on the Light of Life, Jesus, your body is filled with the light He is, and that makes your life rich in spiritual things.

The second part of this section is not good. It deals with an option that you have and face everyday. 23 **But if thine eye be evil, thy whole body shall be full of darkness. If therefore the light that is in thee be darkness,**

how great *is* that darkness! Jesus has flowed "**light**" into everyone to a certain degree. In John 1:9 He said He is "**. . . the true Light, which lighteth every man that cometh into the world**" Sadly, everyone isn't displaying that light.

The word "**evil**" carries the idea of something *that has become hurtful*. Thus, it degenerates to the point of causing pain. It had the potential of God's glory, but it is not seen because the life vision of the person is not on God and His purpose.

If your earthly treasures are not toward Jesus, then your heart is not, which means your spiritual vision is darkened. When that happens to a person, he/she uses the life and resources God has given to him/her for earthly reasons and misses the eternal purpose He has in mind-- His Son's glory.

After that teaching, Jesus gave the most powerful statement that challenges everyone. 24 **No man can serve two masters: for either he will hate the one, and love the other; or else he will hold to the one, and despise the other. Ye cannot serve God and mammon** (money). The reason you cannot serve God and money is because a "god" is always treasured by the one who serves that god, and every god demands to be served in its own way. Money and God have different goals for those who serve them. God's goal is His own glory, and money's goal is the glory of those who have their focus (eye) on it.

Jesus wants us to learn to treasure Him so much that all He puts into our lives is "folded together" and focused on Him. God is not against you owning things and having adequate wealth. But, He is against things and wealth owning you.

Would you say there is a "gap" in your life concerning Jesus being the **single** treasure of your vision?

My Journey and a Struggle to Forgive.

As I shared in the introduction, I was very angry over the fact of my sister's rape and the struggles she went through, which led to her tragic death.

God brought me to a choice to forgive or not to forgive. I remember how I was willing to do anything but release those feelings which I held toward that rapist. I felt God had to understand, and I was justified in feeling as I did. My sister, parents, siblings and I paid a great price because of what he did.

Finally, after a long struggle, I realized I had to come to a place to be willing to forgive. It seemed almost every time I studied the Bible and most every sermon I heard, I was spoken to concerning forgiveness. Each time I tried to draw close to Jesus, to walk with Him, He reminded me of my need to forgive. Every disappointment in my life pointed out my sin of bitterness and called me to repent. When God points something out in your life, you don't have to ask what He has said. He speaks loudly and clearly when He calls you to repentance.

The problem was I tried to forgive, but I could not tell if I had forgiven or not. Sometimes I felt I had and at other times I felt I had not. I had to come to grips with the fact that forgiving **did not** mean I approved of, in any way, what had been done. But, it did mean I had to believe God was in control, and somehow He would work all of this for the good of His children. Looking at those events from one side, I can't see any good in them. If I could go back and change those things, I would. Although, I can see many good things that I would not change that came out of those horrible events. As a result of the way God used our sufferings, many in my family were saved, including me.

To make a long story short, I cried out to God in my weakness, and He worked forgiveness in my heart. How did I know forgiveness had come? To that point, not many days went by that I did not think of the events concerning my sister. My memories of her were boxed in two events, the rape and suicide, which fed my bitterness. (This may not be the same for everyone, but this is how it happened with me).

As I prayed and confessed my bitterness, and asking God to help me forgive, I found myself able to pray that He would forgive the one who had done such evil. By building my life and thoughts on Jesus, my desires changed to His desires for me. Then, I wanting to forgive every offender, because that is what He wants for me. As I learn and understand what matters the most in life is walking closely with Jesus, I want to forgive. As I learn to treasure Him more and more in response to His love for me, I am enabled to do His will.

Now (2018), twenty-one years after writing the first draft of this book (1997), God continues to teach me about His High Purpose for my life. It overwhelms me to think that God wants me, as part of the bride for His Son. He wants me, and you, and is working in us to make us a fit companion for Jesus. He will not stop working in us until we are the pure, blameless, spotless bride that He has planned. Just think, when He finishes with us, we will be fully dressed in His Son's own righteousness. Focusing on these lofty thoughts makes me want to forgive even more than before, and I hope you do too.

By knowing and believing God loves me unconditionally (1 John 4:16 &19), I strive to stay in the process of turning my heart to Him. I can know if my heart is toward Him, because when it is, I choose to freely forgive my offenders. I now experience freedom of thought concerning that rapist. I do not know him, and have not tried to find him. I have left him to God. Forgiving wasn't only something I needed to do years ago, I have to do that almost every time I think about those things. The freedom I have now in Jesus makes me so grateful He helps me forgive.

After being willing to forgive, I was able to go longer periods without thinking of the bad events. I was able to focus on the good things of life. That is how it worked in me. I can honestly say, as much as I hate what was done, I hold no bitterness toward him. If it were not for the grace of God, I know myself well enough to know I could have been just like him or any other evil person. How wonderful it is to be saved!

Did forgiving that man mean I no longer cared for my sister and family? <u>Certainly not</u>. Did it mean I approved of what happened? <u>No</u>, <u>never</u>. It meant I wanted to please Jesus enough to die to myself, my selfish desires. It meant I understood my bitterness was hurting Jesus and me, but not that man. Romans 12:19 **Dearly beloved, avenge not yourselves, but rather give place unto wrath: for it is written, Vengeance is mine; I will repay, saith the Lord.** And, Luke 6:27 **But I say unto you which hear, Love your enemies, do good to them which hate you, 28 Bless them that curse you, and pray for them which despitefully use you.**

I purposed to believe Romans 8:28 **And we know that <u>all things</u> work together for good to them that love God, to them who are the called according to his purpose.**

I am so grateful Jesus' love for me drives my love for Him, out of which I forgive my offenders. I can and do commit those persons and events to God. When I think of my offenders, I pray for them. If I were to have hated anyone of them, you would not be reading this. I would be a castaway concerning a fruitful life and ministry. God speaks to this in 1 Cor. 9:27 **But I keep under my body, and bring it into subjection: lest that by any means, when I have preached to others, I myself should be a castaway** (disqualified).

I am learning how an unforgiving spirit hurts the one who is bitter far more than any other. The more I learn of God's High Purpose for my life, which is to be His Son's companion now and forever, the more I want to live for His pleasure. In this companionship, Jesus displays in me the Greatness of His life-transforming power, so it is Him in me, that make me want to forgive. I know it pleases Jesus when we forgive our offenders, because He prayed for forgiveness for those who tortured and crucified Him. He is working to make us like Himself.

I want to do everything that is best for the one who has done so much for me. By His grace and for His glory, He enables me to forgive. I am free in Jesus to hold no hard feelings toward anyone. I don't like what some have done. Some things still hurt. If Christ can love my offenders, and He does, so should I. It fills my heart with joy to know God is making us like His Son, just like He promised He would do.

1. If you have been reminded of an unresolved conflict where <u>you have bitterness</u>, ask God to forgive you and purpose to forgive your offender. Treasure Jesus enough to forgive (John 14:21 & 23). If you will deeply consider Jesus' love for you, you will respond with growing love for Him and out of your love for Jesus, you will forgive.

2. If you have forgiven those who have hurt you, praise God for His unexplainable grace.

3. How does Jesus' example of freely forgiving those who hurt Him challenge you?

Listen to something the Bible says about Jesus and His suffering. Hebrews 5:8 **Though he were a Son, yet learned he obedience by the things which he suffered;**

My paraphrase: *Though Jesus was God the Son, He learned what compliance to God the Father's will is like from a human standpoint by the suffering He voluntarily endured.*

Jesus knows how painful obedience to God's will can be. He really does understand the pain you endure. Open your heart and talk to Him about your pain.

Week Five, Day One
Walking with God and Learning More about Him.
God Comforts His Hurting Children.

 Memory verse– Ps. 57:7 **My heart is fixed, O God, my heart is fixed: I will sing and give praise.**

The Apostle Paul endured a great trial without losing the victory Christ won for all believers. He came to a place where he thought he would die, or possibly want to, because his stress and troubles were so heavy. Yet he did not depart from the Lord in His heart. 2 Corinthians 1:3 **Blessed be God, even the Father of our Lord Jesus Christ, the Father of mercies, and the God of all comfort; 4 Who comforteth us in all our tribulation, that we may be able to comfort them which are in any trouble, by the comfort wherewith we ourselves are comforted of God. 5 For as the sufferings of Christ abound in us, so our consolation also aboundeth by Christ. 6 And whether we be afflicted, it is for your consolation and salvation, which is effectual in the enduring of the same sufferings which we also suffer: or whether we be comforted, it is for your consolation and salvation. 7 And our hope of you is stedfast, knowing, that as ye are partakers of the sufferings, so shall ye be also of the consolation. 8 For we would not, brethren, have you ignorant of our trouble which came to us in Asia, that we were pressed out of measure, above strength, insomuch that we <u>despaired even of life</u>: 9 But we had the sentence of death in ourselves, that we should not trust in ourselves, but in God which raiseth the dead: 10 Who delivered us from so great a death, and doth deliver: in whom we trust that he will yet deliver us;**

Paul understood his suffering helped him be better able to comfort others who may be in "**any trouble**" (v. 4). He knew his purpose on earth was to demonstrate that Jesus' grace was sufficient no matter what he suffered. Through sufferings he knew he would be able to comfort others more effectively, thus, bring more glory to God. He knew his trials had helped him learn to trust God more, therefore, to trust less in himself (v. 9).

Please understand; when you became a Christian, you entered the ministry (army) of the body of Christ. Being a member of His body subjects you to trials and sufferings. God uses your pain, along with all other things in your life, to conform you to the image of His Son. He makes you more like Jesus for His glory. One way that you can glorify Jesus is by comforting others. Merely being able to comfort others is not a big enough reason to refuse bitterness (when your sufferings are severe) but you being enabled to live in freedom with Jesus certainly is.

You being able to comfort hurting people is extremely important because when their pain seems unbearable, they are fighting spiritual battles, therefore, they need someone like you to help them. They, like us, when in deep pain and suffering can become spiritually confused. A wrong response to suffering can lead to being vulnerable to the dictates of the world, the flesh and evil forces. Hurting people need someone like you who understands the things they are feeling and thinking.

If you are hurting, regardless of why you feel the pain you do, you can be sure God wants to draw you to His heart and to give you comfort. Then, you can use the comfort He gives to help others. Helping others brings glory to Jesus, your most intimate friend and companion. When you lean upon Jesus in faith and love, He uses you to build and expand His kingdom. You can walk with Jesus where you are, if you will.

Point of Truth: God is Good. He wants you to enjoy everything that is holy, wholesome, and healthy, to His glory and for your good. And, all that is unholy, unwholesome and bad for you, He wants you to avoid for His glory and your good.

Through various trials and tribulations, we learn how Christ is sufficient for all things and His ways are best. Our troubles help us lose the desire for this world, so we can focus more on Him. Sometimes we have to lose what our hearts were given to before we can see the need to fix our hearts on Jesus, which is far better for us.

"You'll never know God is enough, until God is all you have."
- Ron Dunn

As you know, God uses difficult circumstances to open the hearts of many so they can see their need for Jesus. Could it be God has you where you are to draw you to His heart, so you can learn to walk more closely with Him?

In verse five, Paul used the word "**abound**" twice. This word "**abound**" can be translated *to exceed, more than can be contained, running over of the cup*. So the verse could be read: *"For as my sufferings for Christ run over the cup, these sufferings are more than I can contain, so the comfort I get from Christ over runs the cup as well, therefore, His comfort is more than I can contain"* (my paraphrase).

Whatever comes into your life as tribulation may be there for a variety of reasons, but certainly Christ wants to be your comfort. He wants you to trust and relate to Him as your own faithful companion.

Notice verse eight. Paul tells of the troubles they endured in Asia. They "**. . . were pressed out of measure, above strength, insomuch that we despaired even of life.**" Paul thought he would die because the pressure was so extreme, yet he was in the center of God's will. It is not strange for a follower of Jesus to be tested, tried, and prepared for a better life, ministry or eternity through sufferings.

Point of Truth: The trials (testings) of life may have come to us from the hand of an enemy. Even so, God takes the things Satan seeks to destroy us with and uses them to mold and make us into the persons He wants us to be.

Saints of God have always, in every generation, endured various kinds of trials. From such testings and trials, you can become mighty in Jesus, IF you respond correctly.

Read verse nine. Why did Paul have this "**sentence of death**," that great heart wrenching trial? "**. . . that we should _____ _____, but in God . . . .**"

Point of Truth: God sharpens the weapon you are for His Son's glory, through the pain you endure at the hands of His enemies.

Jesus told His disciples: John 16:33 **These things I have spoken unto you, that in me ye might have peace. In the world ye shall have tribulation: but be of good cheer; I have overcome the world.** The main emphasis in this verse is not the fact that Jesus' followers will have tribulation, although that is true. The main point is the **peace** and overcoming power we can have in Him during every tribulation.

Jesus does not keep you from every heart wrenching trial. He simply wants to be your source of refuge and comfort in every trial.

When times of severe testing come, there are basically two responses:
1. Repentance and brokenness before God, thus, drawing closer to Him.
2. Hardness of heart and bitterness, thus, pushing away from Him.

Point of Truth: The world, flesh and devil can only do to you what God

allows, but sometimes He allows them to do some very painful things to the most fruitful Christians.

1. What severe adversity has God allowed to come into your life? _____ _____ Most have suffered trying adversities. You may be suffering severely now.

2. Are you hardening your heart against God because of your suffering? _____ If so, ask Him to forgive you and to soften your heart in repentance toward Him.

3. Is there a bitterness in you, that you refuse to release? _____ If so, are you aware it is standing between you and Jesus, you and the comfort God has for you? _____

4. Are you practicing doing all you do each day as unto Christ, and not as unto men? _____

> "The way in which you endure that which you must endure is more important than the crisis itself." -Sam Rutigliano
> Endnote #10, p. 288.

But as we were allowed to be put in trust with the gospel, even so we speak: not as pleasing men, but God, which trieth our hearts.
1 Thessalonians 2:4

Week Five, Day Two
Walking With God and Learning More about Him.
An Example of Faithfulness During Severe Adversity.

 Memory verse– Ps. 57:7 **My heart is fixed, O God, my heart is fixed: I will sing and give praise.**

From your Bible, read the first two chapters of the book of Job.

What type of person was Job? Job 1:1: **". . . was <u>perfect</u> and <u>upright</u>, and one that <u>feared</u> God, and <u>eschewed</u>- (avoided) evil."**

The word "**perfect**" means *complete or whole*.

Job was a man after God's heart, therefore, he could not be shaken from his faith, even though he suffered the loss of almost everything.

Some people have turned away from faithfulness to God when they suffered. The fact that Jesus did not have their hearts was revealed by their reaction to suffering. Had their hearts been fixed on Him, they would have remained faithful, thus clinging to Him.

God allows His followers to suffer for many reasons, and only He knows why. Sometimes we live with questions we never get answers to in this life. That is when we must trust Him.

Job's life illustrates how God accomplishes many things when He allows sufferings. One thing is God proved to Satan that Job served Him because he truly loved Him and not because of the things He had given to him. Job 1:9 **Then Satan answered the LORD, and said, Doth Job fear God for <u>nought</u>? 10 Hast not thou made an <u>hedge</u> about <u>him</u>, and about his <u>house</u>, and about <u>all</u> that he <u>hath</u> on every side? thou hast blessed the work of his hands, and his substance is increased in the land. 11 But, put forth thine hand now, and touch <u>all</u> that he <u>hath</u>, and <u>he</u> will <u>curse</u> thee to thy face.**

Along with proving Job's love was pure, God also uses the book of Job to comfort and encourage His people. Almost everyone has suffered without understanding why. We know suffering purifies the heart when one responds correctly. However, if one responds with long term anger and resentment, thus, does not come to brokenness and humility before God, he/she is likely to develop a hard and bitter heart and reap continuing consequences. Times of suffering reveal the true spiritual condition of a person's heart.

Job understood the danger of allowing his heart to become hardened against God. Speaking about God, he said in Job 9:4 **He is wise in heart, and mighty in strength: who hath hardened himself against him, and hath prospered?**

Your spiritual enemies expect you to harden your heart when you suffer. Don't allow them to be right. Like Job, show your enduring trust in Jesus.

When you go through trials and remain faithful, you discover you really do trust God. You may think you trust Him fully, but a great trial can be used to convince you that your faith is genuine. As you become convinced in your faith, you have more boldness about God and truth. Others will also be convinced of your faith as they watch you maintain your integrity. At times, those who have gone through some of the darkest trials become God's most usable and fruitful servants.

Let's examine how God allowed Job to be tested in different ways. Notice Job's finances were plundered by enemies: Job 1:14-15, 17. When other persons do us harm, we seem to understand more readily because we know people can do and be evil, although the pain and loss is still felt. But, notice how other persons were not the entire problem concerning Job's losses. Job 1:16: **". . .The <u>fire</u> of <u>God</u> is fallen from heaven, and hath burned up . . ."**

What do you suppose Job thought about this? He had to be devastated.

Notice the next report. Job 1:18 **While he *was* yet speaking, there came also another, and said, Thy sons and thy daughters *were* eating and drinking wine in their eldest brother's house: 19 And, behold, there came a great wind from the wilderness, and smote the four corners of the house, and it fell upon the young men, and they are dead; and I only am escaped alone to tell thee.** This was, no doubt, the most difficult. Again, there was not a person to blame. Those heartrending events appeared to be from God. Most people would give all they have and even their own lives for their children's welfare. Was Satan right about Job? Did He curse God? _____ The enemy will accuse you of things of which he is wrong. He will lie to you about circumstances, other persons, yourself, and he will certainly lie to you about God and His purposes for you. He doesn't want you to believe that you are Jesus' companion and how much He loves you, so He lies to you.

What did Job do at the loss of all things (1:20-22)? "**. . . fell down upon the ground, and <u>worshipped</u>**." "**. . . <u>blessed</u> be the name of the Lord.**" "**In all this Job <u>sinned</u> not, nor <u>charged</u> God <u>foolishly</u>.**" What a heart for God this man of faith had. Notice the next attack (2:4-8). Job suffered the loss of his finances, family, and then his flesh was covered with disease. How do you suppose Job felt? _____ How do you think his wife felt (2:9)? _____ She appeared to be angry and bitter. Did Job agree with her (2:10)? _____

Job also lost support of his friends. Job's closest friends accused him of bringing those things about by some secret sin (see Eliphaz-4:7-10; Bildad-8:1-6; Zophar-11:4-5). They believed and propagated lies about Job. Have you witnessed a brother or sister go through severe suffering and secretly asked yourself, "I wonder what God is punishing him/her for?" _____ This can be man's way of viewing others when they are in trouble. Job's friends did that to him. Job needed comfort from his friends, not accusations. Job's wife was bitter. His friends became "know-it-alls" with all of the answers. And the answer from each was, "Job, you are no good. It's all your fault. You brought this on yourself through some secret sin." Notice Job's reply: Job 13:15 **Though he** (God) **<u>slay</u> me, yet will I <u>trust</u> him: but, I will <u>maintain</u> mine own ways before <u>him</u>.** Job continued to trust God even though he went through horrendous, tragic sufferings.

One of the most insightful passages in the book of Job is 42:7-10.

7 And it was so, that after the LORD had spoken these words unto Job, the LORD said to Eliphaz the Temanite, My wrath is kindled against thee, and against thy two friends: for ye have not spoken of me the thing that is right, as my servant Job hath. 8 Therefore take unto you now seven bullocks and seven rams, and go to my servant Job, and offer up for yourselves a burnt offering; and my servant Job shall pray for you: for him will I accept: lest I deal with you after your folly, in that ye have not spoken of me the thing which is right, like my servant Job. 9 So Eliphaz the Temanite and Bildad the Shuhite and Zophar the Naamathite went, and did according as the LORD commanded them: the LORD also accepted Job. 10 And the LORD <u>turned the captivity of Job, when he prayed for his friends</u>: also the LORD gave Job twice as much as he had before.

God would not accept the worship of Job's friends until Job prayed for them. They had not spoken the truth about God and Job. They believed things about God and His ways of working that were incorrect. Wrong belief led them to wrong actions, attitudes, and words. They misunderstood God and what He was doing. It is knowing God's Word, Truth, that makes your opinions right and powerful. They, also, believed lies about Job. They were sure his troubles were self-inflicted through secret sins.

I can picture those guys saying something like this to one another: "How could we have been so wrong? I thought we understood the way God works." I can also see them saying to Job: "We were wrong about God and you, and He is displeased with us. He will not accept our worship until you pray for us. Will you please pray for us?" According to verse 10, had Job recovered when he was asked to pray for his friends? _____ No, he was at his lowest point. Think about how hard it might be for you to pray for your friends if they had accused you of causing the loss of all things, including the death of your children, by you having harbored some secret sin. It would be very difficult. But if you are striving to have your heart fixed on Jesus, to treasure Him above all things, you will forgive and pray for those who hurt you because He commands you to do so.

Point of Truth: You will do what Jesus wants when He means that much to you.

This act of forgiveness was a call to Job to continue to walk with God. It is no coincidence that as soon as Job prayed for his friends, God **turned** his **captivity** (v. 10).

God is speaking to us in these things. Praying for those who have hurt you is for your good. God will test each of us in different ways. You will be tested, or have been tested, or are being tested now. If you don't trust God, you will see your lack of trust in Him. If you do trust Him and draw closer to Him, you will pass the test, and He will restore your heart by revealing more of Himself to you. He will be your comfort, help, and healing. He is always the reward of your faith, and when you have Him, you have more than needed to shine in His glory.

Notice God gave Job **twice as much as he had before** (v. 10). Take note of the fact that Job only received ten more children. But, today in heaven Job has twenty children. God could not replace those ten children, because every person is unique and irreplaceable. Another ten children couldn't replace the relationship he had with each of the ten he lost. And that is how you are to God, too. You are unique and special to Him. He made you for Himself.

God brought Job to a point of forgiveness, a point of turning. When you obey God, He does what He has promised. We should expect no less from God than for Him to keep His promises. If, in this life, you don't see all He has promised, you will in heaven. God is faithful!

Job is an example to us of faithfulness during severe adversity. Are you?

Point of Truth: You can trust God concerning your losses.

1. Do you harbor hatred in your heart toward anyone? _____ If you do, please forgive. You cannot continue to grow spiritually if you refuse to forgive. God will not bless you as He desires as long as you have unforgiveness in your heart. And, you will continue to suffer the consequences as long as you refuse to forgive.

2. Thank God for calling you to forgive others so you can walk more closely with Jesus and be free from the destructive bondage of bitterness.

3. As you treasure Jesus more, you will find forgiving is not as difficult as you thought. If you do not forgive, then you know you have not turned your heart to Him as He desires.

> "There is a living God: He has spoken in the Bible. He means what He says and will do all He has promised."--Hudson Taylor

Week Five, Day Three
Walking with God and Learning More about Him.
An Example of Unfaithfulness During Severe Adversity.

 Memory verse– Ps. 57:7 **My heart is fixed, O God, my heart is fixed: I will sing and give praise.**

Today we will study about a huge failure by King Saul during a time of adversity. 1 Samuel 13:7 **And some of the Hebrews went over Jordan to the land of Gad and Gilead. As for Saul, he was yet in Gilgal, and all the people followed him trembling. 8 And he tarried seven days, according to the set time that Samuel had appointed: but Samuel came not to Gilgal; and the people were scattered from him. 9 And Saul said, Bring hither a burnt offering to me, and peace offerings. And he offered the burnt offering. 10 And it came to pass, that as soon as he had made an end of offering the burnt offering, behold, Samuel came; and Saul went out to meet him, that he might salute him. 11 And Samuel said, What hast thou done? And Saul said, Because I saw that the people were scattered from me, and that thou camest not within the days appointed, and that the Philistines gathered themselves together at Michmash; 12 Therefore said I, The Philistines will come down now upon me to Gilgal, and I have not made supplication unto the LORD: I forced myself therefore, and offered a burnt offering. 13 And Samuel said to Saul, Thou hast done foolishly: thou hast not kept the commandment of the LORD thy God, which he commanded thee: for now would the LORD have established thy kingdom upon Israel for ever. 14 But now thy kingdom shall not continue: the LORD hath sought him a man after his own heart, and the LORD hath commanded him to be captain over his people, because thou hast not kept that which the LORD commanded thee.**

Samuel had clearly told King Saul to wait seven days at Gilgal and then he would come and offer sacrifices. In the evening on the seventh day, Saul took things into his own hands and offered the sacrifices which Samuel the prophet was supposed to do. When Saul finished the sacrifices, Samuel arrived and confronted him about the foolish act of disobeying God's will.

Were the prophets the only ones who were permitted to offer sacrifices at that time? No. That restriction was in the Tabernacle and later in the Temple. So, what was the problem? At least two things: First, Samuel told Saul to wait and he would come and offer those sacrifices (v. 8). Secondly, this would have been an offering of promotion for Saul. God would have established Saul's family as Israel's kings forever. 13 **And Samuel said to Saul, Thou hast done foolishly: thou hast not kept the commandment of the LORD thy God, which he commanded thee: for now would the LORD have established thy kingdom upon Israel for ever. 14 But now thy kingdom shall not continue: . . . .** Saul eagerly pushed forward for promotion because his heart was given to the kingdom of God, rather than, the God of the kingdom. It is foolish to seek self-promotion, even in things you know God has for you.
Point of Truth: Time spent waiting on God is for your good, even when it appears He is late.

Saul should have waited. The phrase "**I forced myself**" (v. 12), reveals how Saul went against his new heart. When you know better than to do something, but you do it anyway, you have **forced** your will over God's will.

Saul and David's lives are pictures, examples, and types of God's people. Some, like Saul, have given their hearts to His kingdom, to His work, to the blessings He has provided, thus, they have not kept their hearts on Him. They treasure the "things of God" more than the God who gave the things. While others are more like David, after God's heart. They have given their hearts to the God of the kingdom and are striving to keep them there, thus, they have remained in the process of turning their hearts to Him. Intimacy with Jesus, being a faithful companion to Him, is more important to them than having their own desires fulfilled. They care more about walking closely with Jesus than gaining worldly possessions, fame, or having their fleshly appetites pacified.

Saul worked diligently to keep his kingdom, while David, after being anointed to take Saul's place (1 Sam. 16), refused to kill Saul, although he had opportunities to do so. Saul tried to kill David for years, but David waited on God to promote him to be king.

Point of Truth: You are the only one who can limit God from doing in your life all His Word says He wants to do in you.

No one but you can control your life. King Saul had a heart for being king and he would do anything to keep his position. King David had a heart for God and he would do anything to keep the fellowship intimate.

Both men had tragic failures (sins) in their lives. Yet when Saul repented, he was not restored. When David repented he was restored. Why? <u>Because God looks at the heart</u>. Saul, so-called "repented," in hopes of having his place in the kingdom restored (Read 1 Sam. 15:30). David repented seeking to be restored in fellowship with God. (Read Ps. 51). God did not respond to Saul's repentance, but restored fellowship with David. Saul's repentance was self-centered, while David's was God-centered, thus love-driven.

It is interesting that both men spoke almost the same words when confronted over their sins. Both said, "**I have sinned . . .**" Notice David's repentance after the sin of adultery and murder (Read Psalm 51). David's repentance was from his heart and toward God's heart.

Some "confess sins" with no thought that God has been offended. Their only motive in repentance is to avoid the consequences (present or future troubles). Saul thought he could do just fine as long as he didn't lose his place in his kingdom. David knew he had offended God and needed to be made right with Him above all.

When God chastened David, He required the life of his child and his family would always suffer as a result of the adultery and murder. When David repented he never mentioned the things he lost. Yet, when Saul repented, the first thing he mentioned was being restored in the eyes of the people, his kingdom (1 Sam. 15:30). It appears he only wanted to worship God as a sign to the people.

From your Bible, read the sad story of Saul's rebellion and "so called" repentance (1 Samuel 15:18-35). Saul did not destroy all of the Amalekites and livestock as instructed. He blamed the people until he was forced to admit he was responsible. 1 Sam. 15:21 **But the people took of the spoil, sheep and oxen, the chief of the things which should have been utterly destroyed, to sacrifice unto the LORD thy God in Gilgal.**

Verse 24 **And Saul said unto Samuel, I have sinned: for I have transgressed the commandment of the LORD, and thy words: because I feared the people, and obeyed their voice.** Blaming or shifting responsibility to others is a sure sign one has not accepted responsibility for his/her sins. The kind of "**fear**" Saul spoke of meant he did not want to lose popularity with the people so he did wrong to appease them, because his kingdom had his heart. If his heart had been fixed on God, he would have feared offending

Him.

Saul was personal kingdom (people) driven therefore, not driven by a heart for God. He was not concerned about God's kingdom, but rather, his own. Therefore, he was rejected by God. Look closely at the words of his so called "repentance." 1 Sam. 15:30 **Then he said, I have sinned: yet honour me now, I pray thee, before the elders of my people, and before Israel, and turn again with me, that I may worship the LORD thy God.** (Don't let the words "**thy God**" cause you to think Saul didn't know God. Samuel used the same term in 1 Sam. 13:13 when speaking to Saul).

David, however, was a man after God's own heart. David's repentance dealt with how he had offended God and needed to be restored in fellowship with Him (Ps. 51).

Saul, unlike Job in the previous lesson, did not trust God and remain faithful when adversity struck.

1. What should be the motive for repentance, to keep one's position, possessions, freedom, or to be restored in fellowship with God? _____

2. Have you ever repented more out of fear of loss of things or a position, rather than, seeking to be right with Jesus? _____ It is good to genuinely repent for any reason, but much better when you repent because you understand you need to be made right with God.

3. Write this week's memory verse:_____

A testimony to think about:

After preaching about the heart for three weeks, a mother gave this testimony. "The other night my husband and our four-year-old son were watching television. Our son wanted his dad to play a game with him. As his dad continued to watch TV, our son walked away and mumbled something. His dad asked him what he said. He replied "All I said was, I'll be glad when you get your heart out of that TV."

We were all amazed that a four year old gained that much insight from the messages. Another sobering thought is the fact that children can tell where our hearts are.

"Repentance always brings a man to this point. "I have sinned." The surest sign that God is at work is when a man says that and means it."
Oswald Chambers, Endnote #15, Dec. 07.

"True repentance hates sin, and not merely the penalty, and it hates the sin most of all because it has discovered and felt God's love."
William Mackergo Taylor,
Endnote 10, p. 205

Week Five, Day Four
Walking with God and Learning More about Him.
A Proper Knowledge of God.

 Memory Verse– Ps. 57:7 **My heart is fixed, O God, my heart is fixed: I will sing and give praise.**

Before you can walk with Jesus in the joy of spiritual fruitfulness, you must gain a correct knowledge of Him. One thing a proper knowledge of God produces is trust in Him. Intimacy with Jesus will not be as it could be if you haven't learned He can be trusted in everything.

The book Drawing Closer: (A step-by-step guide to intimacy with God)[5], speaks to some important things. To summarize this book (which is no longer in print) I want to point out six stages of understanding about God.

1. Sovereign God. (Holy, Sovereign) God is in control. Everyone who believes in the God of the Bible believes He is in control. Many unbelievers hold this view of God too, but that does not make them saved. The next knowledge of God one must gain is:

2. He is Savior. At this point a person can be saved by believing in Jesus to the point of receiving Him as one's own Lord and Savior. When a person is first saved, these are the primary views of God he/she holds.

Keep in mind, you should never lose these concepts of God; you simply learn more about Him. The more you increase in the knowledge of God, the more they become blended together. He is all of these and more. As you enjoy your salvation by walking with Jesus in a heart-to-heart fellowship, you come to see God is:

3. A Loving Father. As you mature spiritually, you become more aware of God as your Father. As you continue to seek Him, you increase in understanding the things He has revealed about Himself. By abiding in Jesus and believing His truth, you learn He is:

4. A Faithful Companion. At this point, you no longer view God as being against you in any way. You believe the truth about the goodness of God toward His own. The truth is, God is for you and loves you unconditionally. He wants to flow His Son's life through you for your good and His glory. Once you accept that Jesus is a faithful companion, you seek to draw closer to Him for who He is. At this point you begin to treasure Him as your own "Faithful Companion." Then you see Him as:

5. A Friend. As you discover Jesus' desire to be your friend, your heart is turning more and more to Him as you spend time seeking Him and believing His Word. As you grow, you come to the place to know Jesus is:

6. Your Most Intimate Friend. At this point, you have turned from all known sins as best as you can and are seeking to trust Jesus with everything. You would rather die than deny Him. You do not want to sin because you do not want to hurt or disappoint Him. No one wants to hurt or disappoint his/her most intimate friend. The worst thing about sin is the fact that it disrupts intimate fellowship between Jesus and you.

When you know Jesus as "Your Most Intimate Companion and Friend," you treasure Him far above everything. Like the Apostle Paul, you treasure Him enough to be willing to suffer the loss of all things to gain more knowledge of Him. Philippians 3:7 **But what things were gain to me, those I counted loss for Christ. 8 Yea doubtless, and I count all things but loss for the excellency of the knowledge of Christ Jesus my Lord: for whom I have suffered the loss of all things, and do count them but dung, that I may win**

Christ. Paul counted all things as loss for a more excellent and deeper knowledge of Christ.

Paul treasured Jesus so much that he counted all other things as manure. Paul did not have a problem giving his heart to Jesus. He couldn't get enough of Him. He wanted to walk closely with Jesus with nothing between. He understood how other things can compete for a believer's heart, loyalty, and allegiance, therefore, he considered them as **loss**, even **dung** (manure).

The word "**win**" could be translated *to gain by striving*. Paul did not strive to gain salvation. He clearly taught that salvation is freely given in Jesus. Paul strove to gain a more intimate fellowship with Jesus, to know Him better, to treasure Him more, to have His approval, His smile.

In Romans 8:28-29 we saw God's **calling** of you is for the purpose of you being **conformed** into the **image** of Jesus, for His glory and your greatest good. Romans 8:28 **And we know that all things work together for good to them that love God, to them who are the called according to *his* purpose. 29 For whom he did foreknow, he also did predestinate *to be* conformed to the image of his Son, that he might be the firstborn among many brethren.**

The following passage is very important in gaining a more accurate and growing knowledge of God. Ephesians 1:15 **Wherefore I also, after I heard of your faith in the Lord Jesus, and love unto all the saints, 16 Cease not to give thanks for you, making mention of you in my prayers; 17 That the God of our Lord Jesus Christ, the Father of glory, may give unto you the spirit of wisdom and revelation in the knowledge of him: 18 The eyes of your understanding being enlightened; that ye may know what is the hope of his calling, and what the riches of the glory of his inheritance in the saints.** God wants our minds to be spiritually enlightened so we will **know what is the hope of his calling** of us, which is to His High Purpose of being made like His Son, (Rom. 8:28-30) to display His glory forever.

Notice the next sentence where God says we (**saints**, saved persons) are **the riches of the glory of his inheritance. . ..** Wow! You are **the riches of the glory of** Jesus' **inheritance** and so am I and all other believers.

This exciting truth should drive us in love to strive to live like the new creations we are in Jesus. He created us and saved us to be His glorious bride and companion. Praise the Lord!

The Enduring Word Commentary on verse 18 states, ". . . Paul wanted them to know the greatness of God's inheritance in His people. We usually think only of our inheritance in God, but Paul wanted the Ephesians to understand that they are so precious to God that He considered them His own inheritance.

Several commentators believe that Paul also spoke of God's inheritance in His people in Ephesians 1:11. But that is certainly his idea here, with Paul probably drawing his idea from Deuteronomy 32:8-9 **When the most High divided to the nations their inheritance, when he separated the sons of Adam, he set the bounds of the people according to the number of the children of Israel. 9 For the LORD'S portion is his people; Jacob is the lot of his inheritance.**"

And the Greek scholar, A. T. Robertson wrote on this verse, "Our riches are in God, God's are in his saints."[8] Think of how much God gave to purchase you to be His Son's bride. He gave His best, His Son, and raised Him from the dead to share life in His glory with you forever. Try to imagine, how spectacular you will forever appear as a trophy of His grace (Eph. 2:7).

God looking upon us as a resource of His wealth is an amazing fact. He sees us this way by viewing us in His Son. Jesus makes all of the difference in us. Without Him, we are nothing to look upon, but in Him, we are trophies of His grace. In Him, we are shining, glorious demonstrations of His redeeming power. He isn't finished with us yet, but He soon will be, then we will have in our experience, what He says is true about us now.

You must also know, Ephesians 1:19 **And what is the exceeding greatness of his power to us-ward who believe, according to the working of his mighty power,**. God is not asking you to be the power in you, but rather, we must know all we are to be for Him is by **his mighty power,**.

What did Paul pray these new believers might receive from God according to verse 17? "**. . . may give unto you the spirit of wisdom and revelation in the _____ of _____.**"

Point of Truth: Spiritual insights come by wisdom and revelation and these are given to us when we have a compelling desire to know Jesus more fully so we can be to Him all He wants us to be for His glory.

What do verses 18 and 19 tell will happen when a person receives spiritually revealed knowledge of Jesus? 18 **The eyes of your understanding being enlightened; that ye may _____ what is the hope of his calling, and what the riches of the glory of _____ inheritance in the saints, And what is the exceeding greatness of his power to _____ who believe, according to the working of his mighty power.**" The word "hope" means *confident expectation*. Read verse 18 with this definition in mind.

Having a wrong understanding of God will result in wrong doctrinal conclusions. Some believers have been led astray by teachers who do not have a proper knowledge of God. They think and live like the world revolves around themselves, rather than, Jesus and His glory. When a believer's knowledge of God is incorrect, he/she is open to deception. If you have the idea that God is against you, that He has no plans to bless you, that He will not give you His joy and freedom, then you are deceived about Him.

You should believe God is committed to your present and eternal joy because Jesus died to make you His own, free companion for His glory. Now He lives in you to conform you to His likeness so His life in you can radiate the glorious message of Who He is and His saving power.

Point of Truth: A proper knowledge of God produces in you a deeper desire for Him, to please Him, to be with Him, which always results in love-driven obedience to Him.

Everything changes when you know God loves you unconditionally and has His Highest Purpose in the universe for you, which is a genuine, intimate, eternal, love-driven relationship that displays His Son's glory.

1. Who desires to be your most intimate friend? _____
2. What must one increase in to grow as one should? _____
_____
3. How are you making adjustments in your life to spend quality time in fellowship with Jesus, to increase in knowledge of Him? _____
_____

"Our greatest danger in life is in permitting the urgent things to crowd out the important." -Charles E. Hummel, Endnote 10, p. 328.

Put your name in the following blank. I, _____, am part of the riches of the glory of Jesus' inheritance. Therefore, because of His great, life transforming work in me, and only because of Him, He now finds me to be a precious treasure.

This truth should compel love-driven surrender and obedience to Jesus.

Week Five, Day Five
Walking with God and Learning more about Him.
Increasing in the Knowledge of God Yields Many Rewards.

 Memory Verse– Ps. 57:7 **My heart is fixed, O God, my heart is fixed: I will sing and give praise.**

Increasing in the knowledge of God is imperative in order to grow spiritually. The most rewarding times of Bible study happen when you study to visit with Jesus, to gain greater knowledge of Him. As you intimately interact with Him in His Word, His Spirit gives you that deeper knowledge of Him. An accurate, deeper knowledge of Jesus increases your love for Him, which causes you to turn your heart to Him and as you do, His Spirit transforms your life to be more like Him.

As you increase in knowledge of God, you gain insight into all aspects of your own life and world. True wisdom about everything comes by learning more about the person, works, and ways of God and His perfect and infallible Word.

Colossians 1:9 **For this cause we also, since the day we heard it, do not cease to pray for you, and to desire that ye might be filled with the knowledge of his will in all wisdom and spiritual understanding; 10 That ye might walk worthy of the Lord unto all pleasing, being fruitful in every good work, and increasing in the knowledge of God;** When you live to **please** Jesus out of a love-driven relationship with Him, and that because you are increasing in knowledge of Him, He flows His life unobstuctedly through you, whereby you show His power to gloriously transform a person into His likeness.

Notice what God said about **knowledge** of Him in the following passage. 2 Peter 1:2 **Grace and peace be multiplied unto you through the knowledge of God, and of Jesus our Lord, 3 According as his divine power hath given unto us all things that pertain unto life and godliness, through the knowledge of him that hath called us to glory and virtue:** God's calling of you is to **glory** and **virtue**. Wow! You will be a glorious sight to behold when God finishes His work in you. You will show Jesus' power and love in all you are.

According to verse two, how are **grace** and **peace** multiplied to believers? ". . . through the _____ of God, and of Jesus our Lord." According to verse three, how many **things** has God given to you which **pertain unto life and godliness, through the knowledge of Him** who has called you? _____ _____ You don't gain "**all things pertaining to life and godliness**" in your experience simply because you are saved. Many things God has for you become yours experientially through increasing in knowledge of Him. For you to know Jesus as He desires, you must walk with Him in heart-to-heart fellowship as you learn His Word.

If Jesus gave you His joy and peace while your heart was not fixed on Him, you would be satisfied with a selfish life, thus, content to go no farther with Him in spiritual growth. Without spiritual growth, your life becomes spiritually stagnant and by that loss of intimacy with Jesus, you become a bad example to others. It is not that God doesn't want you to have all He has for you. He is not stingy with spiritual endowments, but He is careful with them.

A believer who strives to grow in the grace and knowledge of God must have a life and heart which treasures Jesus or the world will get a wrong message about Him. When He is not the focus of one's heart, it can appear that Jesus exist for us, rather than we for Him. God is very concerned about what we believe and demonstrate before people concerning Him.

And, if one claims intimacy with God while refusing to repent of known sins, he/she is doing damage to the cause of Christ. If one truly desires to be His intimate friend, he/she must take bold steps to be as pure in life as possible and that flowing out of a love-driven relationship with Him.

Are you striving to live a pure life for Jesus because you are increasing in knowledge of Him? _____ This means you are learning how deeply He loves you and in response to His love, you love Him, therefore you don't want to disappoint Him. Is your striving to do right driven by love for Jesus, to bless Him, or is it of some lesser compulsion, such as, merely wanting Him to bless you with more things?

To walk with Jesus as He desires, you have to make some important life choices. You must refuse to live in ways that make God appear as though He approves of sins. Jesus died to free us to live high and purposeful lives that display His glorious, redeeming power, not lives entangled in sins, which look like the world around us.

1. Write this week's memory verse _____
_____
2. Pray for your church family's leaders by name, then read the following.

My Journey and Learning More About How God Works With Us.

Over these weeks of study, I have shared some things about my life and how God is bringing me along in my journey.

The following is a mixture of my remarks and a testimony of a lady, named Lorey. Lorey and I hope her testimony helps others facing similar struggles. My remarks are in italics.

In February 1997, three months after Dad's death, I began a word study in the Bible on the word "heart." I was hurting badly over Dad's extended suffering and death. Something amazing took place that I did not know about until late May.

As I studied, God began to work in my heart in a deep way. I found myself becoming more and more free from the bondages (anger and frustration), that I had grown up with. As I studied, I became so captivated with the word study that I began getting up as soon as I awoke. I would begin studying between 3:00 A.M. and 5:00 A.M. I would study seeking to learn what God had to say about my heart. Sometimes, I studied all day and into the night. I studied the 943 uses of the word "heart" very quickly. I was captivated by what I was discovering.

For many years I had asked God to help me understand why there was so much conflict in my life, ministry, and in His church in my generation. It was easy to see how many who were deeply committed to places of service in His church were the same ones doing the most damage to it (very often through struggles for power). As I studied about the heart, I began to see what had driven me and others to conflict. The places of service had our hearts. We meant well, but we were misguided as we sought to be the persons we knew we should be.

Upon completing the word study, I had written more than 100 pages of notes, which I used to write this study.

In late May, Lorey walked into my office and shared an amazing testimony with me. She said, "Back in February God began waking me in the early morning hours to pray for you. I had no idea you were writing a book. All I knew was I was being burdened to pray for you. I would get up sometimes as early as 3:00 A.M. and begin praying for you."

Lorey had no way of knowing that at those same hours I was several miles away in my home writing this workbook.

I want you to read her story. I used her own words for the title:

Always Torn

A few weeks ago you asked me to share with you in written form some of the facts surrounding the burden God gave me to pray for you back in early 1997. Since your request, I have been asking God to give me the right words to express how He has worked so mightily in my life through all of this and especially the workbook. (*I gave Lorey a copy of the rough draft after it was written. She helped make copies at the church office before it was printed the first time*).

I want to share two things. As you already know, when I was a child (3rd grade) my parents divorced. I was very close to my dad. My sister and I were the only two children. I was the one who went hunting with Dad, to work with Dad, reloaded ammunition for the guns, and whatever else Dad did, I did.

I remember near the end of their marriage, I would lay in bed at night and listen to them fight. Dad would leave, but he was always home in time to take me to school the next morning. No matter what they fought over, I knew he loved me because he always came back.

Then, one day I was told my sister and I would be moving to another state with Mom. It was very difficult for me, but as children do, we made adjustments.

I found myself not only away from Dad, but Mom began working two jobs and attending nursing school. Often, everything about a child's life changes after divorce.

I would see Dad for a month or so in the summer. You get two of each holiday when your parents are competing with one another; Two birthdays, Easters, Christmases, always one parent trying to outdo the other. Dad was always able to do more because Mom was struggling to make ends meet.

Then there was school and Sunday School. When you make a special thing, to whom do you give it, Mom or Dad, always torn? Always torn, not wanting to hurt someone's feelings. Divorce is so sad, but as a child you just learn to roll with the punches and do whatever you are told.

However, when I reached the age of 30, the fact of my parent's divorce devastated me. At first I thought I was going crazy. I couldn't believe something that took place so long ago could be so difficult for me now. My dad, the one I loved so much, had made a decision to leave me and love and raise someone else's children instead of me.

My stepmother had two daughters that had gained my dad. My dad gave both of them away at their weddings, but told me he was unable to come to my wedding because of a big business meeting. I called him the day after my wedding to let him know how things went. I found he was on vacation with my stepmom. I never told him I knew. That really devastated me. That pain grew and grew inside of me until I became physically ill.

My emotionally induced illness grew worse after I had committed to pray for you. When I would drive to a nearby town to take care of regular errands, often I would have to pull over and stop for awhile because I was sobbing so that I could not drive. I share all of this because I now really believe you were at the point in the workbook that God was going to use to help me find victory over all of that. Although, I didn't even know you were writing a book at that time.

I didn't know why I was praying for you. I was praying that God would give you wisdom, that He would keep your heart and mind focused on Him, that He would protect you and your family. I just prayed. I believe now that I was praying and praying so hard for you because you were at a point in the book that God was going to use to show me how to overcome this devastation. God knew I needed the words He was giving to you, so He spoke to my heart to lift you up in prayer.

While working through the study, I had to stop and write to my dad. God allowed me to let go of that hurt, to love my dad again like I did as a little girl so long ago. Only my heavenly Father could ever know what it meant to me to put all of that to rest. I thank God for using you as an instrument in your writing. I continue praying daily that God will always have your heart completely and that He will continue to give you wisdom. I pray that He will truly bless you and your family.

The second thing that I want to share dealt with my coming before God and asking for forgiveness. I had developed a strong bitterness toward my father-in law. This too, was part of the emotional struggles that had made me physically ill. When I would discover he was coming to visit, I would have to begin taking medication for my stomach. I truly did not like him. I was not hateful to him, but I certainly did not go out of my way to make him feel comfortable.

When I went through the workbook, I thought I was going to be required by God to ask my father-in-law to forgive me and I didn't know how I was to do that because he didn't know how I felt. As I worked through the workbook, God showed me that I was to ask only God for forgiveness and begin respecting authority. When I asked God, correction, when I begged God to please forgive me and let me love this man, it was like someone literally lifted me up. Such a heavy feeling was gone.

Something amazing took place that I did not plan. The next time I saw my father-in-law, I actually went to the door and hugged him when he came in. It shocked me and there is no telling what he must have thought.

I was once told that if you have a burden to pray, but don't know what God wants you to pray about, just ask Him and whatever He brings to your mind, pray about that. When I asked God what He wanted me to pray for, He placed your name in my heart. Sometimes, as early as 3:00 a.m., and almost every morning, I would wake up and I couldn't go back to sleep so I knew I was awake for a reason. So, I would pray for you.

One morning in church, after I had been praying for you daily, you shared how one of the ladies who was in the nursing home, one who faithfully prayed daily for you, had died. When you shared how you needed someone to take her place in prayer for you, at that moment, God clearly spoke to my heart about that matter. I have been called by God to pray for you. It was interesting because I had already been praying for you.

You had shared how someone may be in a position where he/she can do the most good in God's work by praying for others. For a long time, I didn't say anything to you about the way I had been praying for you because I knew once I told you, I would be responsible to continue and I wasn't sure I was responsible enough to make that kind of commitment to God and you. However, I did not stop praying for you.

When you shared about the book, I prayed for you. When you shared that you might be leaving the church, I prayed for you and your family. When you took on the new position that has enabled you to be used to touch more lives, I prayed for you.

In Christ, I love your wife, your children and you. I continue to pray that

God will love all of you, protect you, bless you, and continue to use you.

I'm so glad God gave me the courage to tell you that I had been praying for you. Now I understand why I was praying for you at all hours of the day and night. I was praying for you while you were writing the book that God was going to use to help me become victorious in those desperate areas of my life. If you had not listened to God at times like 3:00 a.m. or 5:00 a.m., I might still be struggling today. Thank you for listening and writing as you did.

I am so thankful for the closeness I now have with Jesus. I know He could not let me grow with all of that bitterness in me. What a wonderful Heavenly Father we have.

As I read Lorey's testimony, I realized that this work was being accomplished by more than myself. If Lorey had not obeyed and prayed, I wonder where this work would be, or if it would be at all.

It will take another world to see who really made the differences down here in God's work. I believe with all that is in me that prayer is the most important part of our participation with God as He works in the world. I believe the major thing holding revival back is a revival of prayer by those whose hearts are fixed on Jesus, thus, they treasure Him above all else. Pray that God will burden us to pray as we never have before. He has already spoken to us through His Word concerning prayer. May we believe His promises and pray and not stop.

2 Chronicles 7:14 **If my people, which are called by my name, shall humble themselves, and pray, and seek my face, and turn from their wicked ways; then will I hear from heaven, and will forgive their sin, and will heal their land.**

"The way to deeper knowledge of God is through the lonely valleys of soul poverty and abnegation of all things."
-A. W. Tozer. Endnote 7, p. 23.
The word "abnegation" means *to deny oneself a right or convenience.*

Week Six, Day One
Subjection to Authority: God's Way to Greatness-- *a godly influence for Jesus.*
God is in Control of All That Happens to You.

 Memory verse– Romans 13:1 **Let every soul be subject unto the higher powers. For there is no power but of God: the powers that be are ordained of God.**

Please make an extra effort to be sure to memorize this week's memory verse.

This week's lessons may contain the most challenging Biblical principles you have encountered. They were for me, because I was very rebellious as a child and still have that tendency wanting its way in me at times.

As I studied God's Word, I was confronted with the truth that a person who pursues Jesus and His righteousness will grow in desiring to be right with Him and all God ordained authorities.

The first thing we must understand, as relating to obeying God ordained authorities, is <u>God is the highest authority</u>. Therefore, what He says overrules all other authorities. What I mean is, if an authority in your life (any person over you in any way) asks or commands that you do something God says you should not do, then it is not rebellion to disobey his/her wishes, but be careful with your attitude as you refuse to do wrong. It is never permissible to do wrong, even when a human authority, organization, or government commands you to do so. Yet, you must humbly resist doing wrong, being careful to not have a rebellious attitude toward those God has placed in positions of authority.

The following passage is extremely important concerning learning about being under authority and being the right kind of person in authority over others. Luke 7:1-10 **Now when he had ended all his sayings in the audience of the people, he entered into Capernaum. 2 And a certain centurion's servant, who was dear unto him, was sick, and ready to die. 3 And when he heard of Jesus, he sent unto him the elders of the Jews, beseeching him that he would come and heal his servant. 4 And when they came to Jesus, they besought him instantly, saying, That he was worthy for whom he should do this: 5 For he loveth our nation, and he hath built us a synagogue. 6 Then Jesus went with them. And when he was now not far from the house, the centurion sent friends to him, saying unto him, Lord, trouble not thyself: for I am not worthy that thou shouldest enter under my roof: 7 Wherefore neither thought I myself worthy to come unto thee: but say in a word, and my servant shall be healed. 8 For I also am a man <u>set under</u> authority, having under me soldiers, and I say unto one, Go, and he goeth; and to another, Come, and he cometh; and to my servant, Do this, and he doeth it. 9 When Jesus heard these things, he marvelled at him, and turned him about, and said unto the people that followed him, I say unto you, I have not found so great faith, no, not in Israel. 10 And they that were sent, returning to the house, found the servant whole** (healed) **that had been sick.**

A "**centurion**" was a Roman military officer over one hundred soldiers. This centurion had been good to the Jews in under his area of command (v. 4-5). Notice this man was <u>little in his own eyes</u> (v. 6-7). He did not perceive himself to be a great man, even though he had great authority. The people told Jesus this man was "**worthy**," but the man did not consider himself as worthy as they saw him (v. 7).

"Nothing sets a person so much out of the devil's reach as humility."
Jonathan Edwards -Endnote 10, p. 308.

The following verse teaches something everyone in a position of authority must know in order to be used by God as He wants. Luke 7:8 says, "**For I also am a man _____ _____ authority. . .**" This man did not say what most leaders would say. Most would say: "I am a man set OVER others; therefore, I tell them to do this or that and they do it." He had an understanding which leads to protection and influence with God and man. He understood the way God has ordained authority to work. He knew his authority was directly connected to his relationship and obedience to those in authority OVER him.

This centurion understood how things work in this world and he was sure it was the same in the spiritual realm and he was right. Many believers need to learn and practice this.

When a person begins to view himself/herself as set OVER those under him/her, he/she loses influence for righteousness, thus runs the risk of functioning as a dictator or tyrant. Some church leaders miss God's plan at this point.

If you violate the principle of submission to authorities, you soon lose godly influence over those under your authority. As you realize you are most influential and powerful when properly related to those above you, you become a mighty instrument in God's hands. Some will not surrender and submit to God and the authorities He has ordained over them, because such surrender means death to one's own desire to be in control. However, a submissive follower gets to walk closely with Jesus and He demonstrates His power through him/her.

Notice how Jesus responded to the Centurion's insight about authority. Luke 7:9 **When Jesus heard these things, he _____ at him, and turned him about, and said unto the people that followed him, I say unto you, I have not found so great faith, no, not in Israel.**

Should you obey and submit to your authorities no matter the costs (as long as they do not command that you violate God's Word)? ____ Humble submission to your authorities opens the door for Jesus to freely flow His fruitful life through you, thus revealing how powerful His glorious life in you is. The costs associated with being under authority are good investments in your life and future.

Did that centurion have influence with soldiers under him? ____ Did he have voluntary influence with the Jews under him? _____ Did He have influence with Jesus because of his understanding of submission to authority that led to his strong faith? ____ Was God glorified through him? _____
Point of Truth: Understanding of, and obedience to truth results in deeper insights and more faith.

The Roman Centurion understood how he must obey those over him or he could not expect those under him to obey his commands. His faith that those under him would obey him was based on his relationship to those **over** him. He expected those soldiers to obey because he was rightly related to Caesar, the Roman emperor. If he were not in the military, under the authority of a higher command, he would have had no faith the lowest ranking soldier would obey him. 1. In what area/s have you been challenged to seek to become more submissive to those over you? _____

_____
2. What does Jesus typically find when He examines your attitude toward

those He has placed over you, submission or rebellion? _____

3. Do you suppose Jesus finds more pleasure and glory in believers who have so much faith in Him that they submit to their authorities? _____

4. In many families and church families there is an element of rebellion to authority. Our society is plagued with many who have a rebellious attitude. They are quick to oppose anyone in authority, unless the person in authority does what they want. How might God use you to help others avoid rebellion? _____

5. Would you say you are or are not humble enough to submit to your God ordained authorities? I am or I am not. Circle one.

Know this, there is most often a gap between where you are spiritually and where God is calling you. He is calling you to humbly submit to those over you. If you are not, will you, now, choose to submit to your authorities? _____

6. If you have rebelled against a church leader/s in the past, ask God if He wants you to apologize to them and maybe even to your church family (be sure to speak with your pastor about how and when to do this)? Your apology and commitment to no longer rebel could be what God uses to spark fires of revival.

7. If Jesus wants you to apologize to someone, for His glory, will you do it? _____

Your church family needs many godly examples of those who understand that submission to authorities is submission to God Himself, therefore, submit for His glory. Let the world see Jesus in you by your humble submission.

8. What do you suppose might happen if everyone in your church family became extremely careful in relating to every authority in his/her life? ____ _____

One great thing that would definitely happen is God would be pleased. That is enough, if nothing else were to take place.

9. The most important thing going on in the universe, as relating to your life, is what God is saying to you now. What is He saying to you? _____ _____

10. Pray for everyone in authority over you, which includes your pastor, staff, deacons and all other church leaders.

11. How do you think the bride of Christ should conduct herself (of which you are a part)? _____

Week Six, Day Two
Subjection to Authority: God's Way to Greatness-- *a godly influence for Jesus.*
Avoiding a Wrestling Match That You Can't Win.

 Memory verse– Romans 13:1 **Let every soul be subject unto the higher powers. For there is no power but of God: the powers that be are ordained of God.**

2 Samuel 22:27 **With the pure thou wilt show thyself pure; and with the froward thou wilt show thyself unsavoury.** The word "**pure**" is used two times in this verse. Both English words were translated from the same Hebrew word. King David had learned when a person is "**pure**" God will reveal Himself to him/her in **pure** ways. The word **pure** means *to make clear, to brightly polish*. God says He will make Himself <u>clear, brightly polished</u> to each one who makes himself/herself <u>clear, brightly polished</u>.

When you take the necessary steps in striving to present your life pure before God, He will allow you to clearly see Him at work in your life. This means life makes sense to the one who is striving to be <u>pure</u> in heart and life. (Unless God is refining him/her for a time. There may be times when life is confusing to the most faithful and pure. During those times one must follow by faith. There will be times when you cannot <u>trace</u> God, so you must <u>trust</u> Him by faith alone).

In general, the pure in heart will be able to see what God is doing in his/her life enough to faithfully endure in both good and hard times. Jesus said, Mattthew 5:8 **Blessed are the pure in heart: for they shall see God.**

To experience personal revival, your heart must remain in the process of becoming **pure**. Jesus said in John 14:21 **He that hath my commandments, and keepeth them, he it is that loveth me: and he that loveth me shall be loved of my Father, and I will love him, and will <u>manifest myself to him</u>.** The "manifested presence of God" often happens when a person becomes broken over sins and turns to God welcoming His presence by loving Jesus so much that he/she strives to obey His will no matter the costs.

No one can tell exactly how God will express Himself when He visits a person in such a way, but you can be sure there will be a burning desire to get as right with Him as one can. And when right, there is confidence that gives inner calmness, a real peace.

However, life to the disobedient will become confusing, complex, and vain. Life to the obedient is insightful, revealing, and there is a confident expectation that God will make all things, even painful things, work out for good. The obedient one automatically looks for God's handprints on every event of life, both good and bad. While the disobedient cannot see surpassing good in life even when things are calm. Those with pure hearts toward God have the strength and spiritual ability to make sense of life, while those in rebellion live in confusion much of the time. God allowing a person to make sense of life produces peace of mind, while confusion tends to lead to anger, frustration, worry, fear, anxiety, depression and such.

Having a God given understanding that He is in control and He is working all things for our good and His purposes, gives confidence about life and helps us make wise decisions which result in our good and His glory.

Notice the second part of 2 Sam. 22:27, **"and with the froward thou wilt show thyself unsavoury"** The word "**froward**" means *distorted; hence false:--crooked, perverse*. When a person will not become "**pure**" thus, open and transparent before God concerning his/her desires, motives and sins, he/she is being **froward**. The word "**unsavoury**" means *to twine, to struggle, to wrestle.* God will *struggle* or *wrestle* with His child who will not heartily surrender to Him and His will or honestly deal with his/her known sins. Is God wrestling with you at this time? _____ Is He using your circumstances as a wrestling match with you, seeking to bring you to repentance, thus, purity of heart and life where you treasure Jesus more than anything? _____

When God speaks to you about your sins, He expects you to repent and turn from them, thus, polish your life through repentance.

Through turning your heart to God, you are changed into His likeness (2 Cor. 3:15-18). Too much is at stake in Jesus' inheritance (Eph 1:18) for God to allow His followers to not be conformed into His Son's likeness. God will stop at nothing to eternally exalt His Son in every believer.

So, those who brightly polish their lives will see God at work in all things. And, those who refuse to brightly polish their lives will be in confusion and struggle until they surrender to God and His will.

One day God will bring this nation, as He does all nations that turn away from Him, to our knees. May it be through revival, I pray. If His people do not return to Him, He will bring us back one way or the other. We know He will not let things go on forever as they are. There is an epidemic of rebellion in our land and even in many churches. Many believers rebel against church leaders as though it is permissible. Some are even proud of their rebellion by thinking themselves as fearless and bold. When someone, or a group, rebels against church leaders, you must be wise enough to not join them, but rather, oppose the rebellion. God will honor you if you do what is right.

Sometimes church leaders make poor decisions or do wrong things. As you know, no human is perfect. When our leaders make poor decisions, those times serve as opportunities to show Christ's love to everyone involved. We are to move forward in love as the church takes measures to humbly work through every situation. (I am not saying leaders are not to be dealt with when they do wrong. I am saying, we should deal with them humbly and respectfully when that is necessary).

When you refuse to rebel, you are showing faith in God because you know He will use all things for your good. God will honor you when you cannot honor a person who holds a position, but you honor him/her anyway because of the position God has allowed him/her to hold. David honored King Saul, even though Saul wasn't always honorable. The times David did dishonor Saul, he repented.

God is wrestling with many, seeking to bring them to repentance and personal revival. May we, by His grace, cling to Him in prayer until revival takes place in our land. What must take place for Biblical revival to happen? God said, "**. . . Return unto me, and I will return unto you, saith the LORD of hosts . . .**" Malachi 3:7.

Each one of us, if we have not, can return to God for personal revival. To do so, we must get right with Him, which includes striving to get as right as we can with others, especially those He has placed over us.

1. If God is calling you to serve Him in a particular ministry, surrender and submit to His will now. If He is, write it here: _____

2. If there is an area in your life which needs to be brightly polished by repentance, thus, departure from a particular sin, repent and confess it.

3. Ask God to teach you more of His truth about being submissive to the authorities He has placed over you.

> "As we begin to focus upon God, the things of the Spirit will take shape before our inner eyes." --A. W. Tozer, Endnote 7, p. 53.

A clear illustration of the rebellion that exists in America is the way people often respond to coaches, referees and umpires. They are in those positions of authority and should be treated with respect, even when they fail or do wrong. God will justly deal with them as He will all others.

Sporting events are a perfect stage for believers to demonstrate respect for authority. Remember, others are watching us, including our children.

Do you need to change the way you respond to coaches, referees or umpires?

Week Six, Day Three
Subjection to Authority: God's Way to Greatness-- *a godly influence for Jesus.*
Winning an Important Decision in God's Court.

 Memory verse– Romans 13:1 **Let every soul be subject unto the higher powers. For there is no power but of God: the powers that be are ordained of God.**

In 1983, I heard for the first time a clear presentation of the Biblical teachings of Submission to God Ordained Authorities. I was amazed by what I heard. I knew it was the truth. I could see how my life had suffered because of my rebellion to God and the authorities He had placed over me. I also came to believe if I would get right with my authorities, God would bless me through them and He has abundantly.

This week's memory verse deals with **powers**, rulers, and authorities. It is referring primarily to government authorities. What is true of subjection to government authorities is also true of all authorities. The principle of submission to authorities is always in effect.

The word "**powers**" (memory verse) was translated from the Greek word "exousia," it means *mastery, influence, authority*. It is sometimes translated "authority," such as: 1 Corinthians 15:24 **Then cometh the end, when he shall have delivered up the kingdom to God, even the Father; when he shall have put down all rule and all authority-(exousia) and power.**

All persons over others in God approved ways have been placed there by Him. From presidents, kings, officials, and all other rulers, to the dads and moms in the smallest families, God has set them in the world as it has pleased Him. He uses the righteous and the wicked to work out His plans and purposes.

God is the supreme authority. Rom. 13:2 **Whosoever therefore resisteth the power, resisteth the ordinance of God: and they that resist shall receive to themselves damnation.**" The Greek word translated "**damnation**" means *to lose a decision of the court*.

In your opinion, does "**whosoever**" include you? _____ The word "**resisteth**" means *to stand against, to oppose*. It does not mean disagree. You may disagree with an authority and be right about the issue, but you must not stand in rebellious opposition to that authority when disagreeing, for rebellion is sin. When you disagree with an authority, it must be done in humility with a quiet spirit or you will be found guilty of rebellion. You can be right about an issue, but wrong in attitude when disagreeing.

"God calls us to represent His authority, not to substitute His authority."
-Watchman Nee, Endnote 14, p. 118

All leaders make some incorrect or poor decisions at times. You must be humble when you disagree with or confront an authority. If you are humble, most persons in authority will come to know you intend only good. God will more likely work through your authorities to help you when He sees you are humble in attitude and actions toward those over you.

Most leaders will be open to your disagreement if you disagree with a submissive attitude. You will have much more influence on your leaders if you are humble, submissive, gentle, and meek. Your opinions carry a lot of influence for Jesus when presented with a submissive attitude.

Point of Truth: You do not submit based on the worthiness of the one in authority. You submit because God told you to, and you know He has a

plan for you and the people over you are part of that plan. So good or evil, strong or weak, wise or foolish, you submit to the person in that position, submitting as unto the Lord.

Your submission is evidence of your devotion to Jesus. In your opinion, would God get more glory from someone who submits to a good, loving leader or a harsh, unreasonable leader? _____
Does a person normally grow more in character during times of ease or during times of adversity?_____ One normally learns and grows more during times of adversity and stress. Which is more important, you being changed into the person God wants or you having an easier way? ___
_____

God uses authorities in key ways to work in His people. Think about this: Some of the persons you have been placed under, where things were difficult, have most likely been used by God to make you more aware of your need of Him. You may be at such a place now. Difficult situations under authorities bring a person to the end of trusting in himself/herself if he/she responds correctly. An incorrect response usually results in anger and bitterness which causes one to reap even more adversity, which tends to result in more rebellion. Rebellion is a downward spiral in a person's life.

God says those who are caught in rebellion to authorities will lose their case before Him. However, even when we have done wrong and we lose the decision in God's court, we can know He is at work in us then too.

Doing right is a choice. You do not have to rebel, therefore, you should not. You should patiently trust God, especially concerning those He has placed in authority over you.

Do you know God cares for you? _____ Do you trust Him? _____ Should you submit to all authorities (as long as they do not command you to violate God's Word) even when you disagree? _____ When you submit to those in authority because you understand God has a purpose for each one in authority, you are actually submitting to God more than the persons. Rom.13:3 **For rulers are <u>not</u> a terror to good works, but to the <u>evil</u>. Wilt <u>thou</u> then not be afraid of the power? Do that which is good, and thou shalt have <u>praise</u> of the same: 4 For he is the <u>minister</u> of God to <u>thee</u> for good. But if thou do that which is evil, be afraid; for he beareth not the sword in vain: for <u>he</u> is the minister of God, a revenger to execute wrath upon him that doeth evil.**

Have you thought of those over you as "**ministers of God**" (v. 4)? ____

"There is no authority except from God; all authorities have been instituted by Him. By tracing all authorities back to their source, we invariably end up with God. . . . In touching God's authority we touch God Himself. God's work basically is done not by power but by authority. . . . All Christians must therefore learn to obey authority." -Watchman Nee, Endnote 14, p.22

One may like to think good, kind, smart, and gentle persons are there for good, but surely not the difficult, harsh, and not so smart. But, they all have been placed in authority by God to be used of Him. God used the following to help me with the principle of submission to authorities.

When I was sixteen years old, my eldest sister moved from Atlanta, Georgia to Arkansas. She had an antique car stored at a friend's house in Atlanta. I went there to drive the 1956 Ford to Arkansas. I discovered the engine needed some repairs before I could leave.

In that community there was a country mechanic. After inspecting the car, he told me it would be ready late the next day. I arrived at the shop as he was completing the repairs. As we talked, I noticed a small oil line circling the top of the engine. I was not familiar with this type of extra oiling system. It looked odd to me. I asked about it. He said, "That is an overhead oiler." I asked, "Is it good this car has that?" He knew I was about to drive the car to Arkansas and I suppose I sounded a little anxious. After some deep thought, he said something I have not forgotten. He said, "Well, it's like this: it ain't good that it needed it, but seeing it needed it, it sure is good its got it."

And that is the way it is with us, because we battle against sinning, especially in times of trouble or temptation. It would be better if we didn't need to be changed, but we do. So, God works those needed changes through all things. He especially works through authorities, good and bad. Seeing we do need to be changed, it sure is good to know God works through all things for our good and His glory. Romans 13:5 **Wherefore ye must needs be subject, not only for wrath, but also for conscience sake. 6 For this cause pay ye tribute also: for they are God's ministers, attending continually upon this very thing.** For what "**cause**" should we be in subjection to those in authority and show our submission by paying taxes? For **wrath** and **conscience sake**. Whose "**ministers**" are they? _____

One normally learns to obey authorities as a child. We learn to obey mostly to avoid "**wrath**" (punishment). But we should mature and obey because we have developed good character and desire to please those in authority, especially God, the highest in the chain of authority.

Point of Truth: A clear conscience is vital for walking in a love-relationship with Jesus.

Slice it any way you wish and you will discover all who rebel against authorities are judged and punished by God. Rebellion to authorities results in a decision in God's court which the rebel never wins. We must strive to maintain a clear conscience in all areas of our lives, including relating to authorities.

Policemen and judges are to execute authority and enforce the law, but they should not write the law themselves. Likewise, those placed in authority merely represent God's authority. Their authority is in a representative capacity, not because they, in and of themselves, are more excellent than the rest of us.

A person might ask, "What about corrupt policemen, judges, and other officials, are they ordained by God?" Yes. He uses the good and the evil to accomplish His purposes, but that does not mean the corrupt get by with their sins. They will stand before God in judgement and they are also reaping the sorrows of their sins in this life as well, even when it appears they are getting by with their sins. No one gets by with committing sins. All sins bring consequences. And, sadly, the unsaved will suffer eternally. The repentant are pardoned from eternal punishment because Jesus bore our sins for us. He absorbed the penalty of our sins in His own body. However, we still reap consequences in this life from our sins. When you repent, God may change or remove the consequences or He may not, that is His decision. Your part is to be the best you can be toward God and His authorities and leave the outcome to Him. Trust Him! Thus, submit to your authorities. God is more likely to change things when your heart and life please Him.

Romans 13:7 **Render therefore to all their dues: tribute to whom tribute is due; custom to whom custom; fear to whom fear; honor to whom honor.** What about paying taxes? It is not always easy to pay taxes. Yet, believers are commanded to do so. High taxes, like corrupt leaders, are used of God to apply pressure upon His people for their good and His purposes. Suffering under corrupt leaders should prompt believers to seek God for Spiritual renewal and awakening. In Biblical history, suffering under evil authorities often drove God's people to repentance, which resulted in their ultimate good.

What might it take to cause America to get back to having our hearts fixed on Jesus, thus respecting our God ordained authorities, which will free us for unhindered fellowship with Jesus?

God works supernaturally through all who return to Him with all of our hearts. If we refuse to return to Him, we will not experience revival. We must be willing to come clean before God in every area of our lives, including submission to Him and the authorities He has ordained.

God has placed you where He wants you. He gave you the parents or guardians and other authorities He wanted you to have. Some may ask: "Why did God allow bad things to happen in my life?" Or, "Why did He allow me to be born into a bad situation at home?" Or, "Why did He allow me to experience the difficult things I have gone through?" Or, "Why did He allow me to have these weaknesses which trouble me so?" Only God can answer those questions. Yet, He has given insight into His way of working in His people. Isaiah 8:11 **For the LORD spake thus to me with a strong hand, and instructed me that I should not walk in the way of this people**.

"Isaiah said the Lord spoke to him 'with a strong hand' that is, by the pressures of circumstances. Nothing touches our lives but it is God Himself speaking." -Oswald Chambers. Endnote 15, Jan. 30.

God is working in us with a glorious, eternal perspective. He views us in a much broader way than we. He allows some things we cannot understand. By faith we can submit to Him and He will work mightily through our weaknesses, scars and hurts.

God put you where He would best be able to get your attention, accomplish His will and reveal the life transforming power of His Son in you. He knew you before you were born. He gave to you your personality and knew what you would be like. He knew the type of person you would be. He also knew the plan He has for you. With these things in mind, He placed you in the family, state, nation, situations, race, gender, etc., that He wanted.

Someone might think "If God had made things easier and more comfortable for me, I would have responded to Him with more obedience." This is not the case. If all you knew were a "bed of roses" in life, you would not be as prone to seek God. Our own experiences show we tend to turn to God in a deeper sense when touched by adversity, pain, and instability.

Please don't misunderstand. God does not do evil. Evil comes from the world, the flesh, and the devil (which He created for His purposes). He knew man would sin; therefore, He designed the world in a way that pleased Him. He uses all things to do His will in breaking hard hearts. It is through breakings and blessings that He rids us of the desire to overly treasure other things. As we mature in Christ, we learn to seek Him more and more because of the blessing of Who He is to us and the great plan He has for us.

1. Is there an area in your life, as relating to authority, where you need to be more submissive? ____ If so, ask God to forgive your rebellion against Him and His authorities.

2. Ask God to teach you more about His truth of submitting to authorities.

3. Put each part of the following verse, which is about church leaders, in your own words. **Obey them that have the rule over you, and submit yourselves:**

for they watch for your souls, as they that must give account, that they may do it with joy, and not with grief: for that *is* unprofitable for you. Hebrews 13:17. **Obey them that have the rule over you-** _____
_____

and submit yourselves-_____

for they watch for your souls- _____

_____

as they that must give account- _____

_____

that they may do it with joy, and not with grief-_____
_____

for that *is* unprofitable for you. _____

"If our idea is that we are being mastered, it is proof that we have no master; if that is our attitude to Jesus, we are far away from the relationship He wants. He wants us in the relationship in which He is easily Master without our conscious knowledge of it, all we know is that we are His to obey.
-Oswald Chambers, Endnote 15, Sept. 22

For promotion cometh neither from the east, nor from the west, nor from the south. 7 But God is the judge: he putteth down one, and setteth up another. Psalm 75:6-7

From where does **promotion** in life originate? _____

Romans 8:28 **And we <u>know</u> that <u>all</u> things work together for <u>good</u> to them that love God, to them who are the <u>called</u> according to <u>his</u> purpose.**

How many things does God work together for good to those who love Him? ___ _____ Whose "**purpose**" is involved in that verse?_____

Knowing God is working **all things together** for your **good** and His **purpose** helps you trust Him in **all things**, especially when you know His **purpose** is for you to glorify Jesus, through which He makes your life full and significant.

Week Six, Day Four
Subjection to Authority: God's Way to Greatness-- *a godly influence for Jesus.*
Sometimes Doing Right Results in Suffering.

 Memory verse– Romans 13:1 **Let every soul be subject unto the higher powers. For there is no power but of God: the powers that be are ordained of God.**

The idea of being submissive and serving others isn't appealing to most, yet God wants us to learn to serve Him and others. In the Bible there are a few Greek words translated into the English word "**servant.**" There are two words used most often. The word used the most is *doulos*. This word is used far more than any other. It means *a slave or bondslave* (bondslave= *slave by choice*). It is often used when describing our service to Christ. The next is the word *diakonos*, which means *minister*. It is a form of the word translated "deacon." Jesus used this word in the following passage. Mark 9:35 **And he sat down, and called the twelve, and saith unto them, If any man desire to be first, the same shall be last of all, and servant of all.** The word *diakonos* "*servant*" describes a believer's service to one another. God says, you become a leader by serving Him and people.

Point of Truth: We are Christ's bond servants (doulos=slaves by choice), therefore, we are His ministers/servants--(diakonos), to His body, the church, and then to the world.

In John 15:15, Jesus said He no longer calls us servants, but now calls us friends. As you function from the platform of friendship and companionship with Jesus, your heart beats for the things He loves and you find yourself desiring to fulfill His will at all costs. Your desire for having a heart for Him is revealed by an increasing desire to serve Him and others for His glory.

There is one type of authority of which God never approves. Matthew 20:25 **But Jesus called them unto him, and said, Ye know that the princes of the Gentiles exercise dominion over them, and they that are great exercise authority upon them.** Do not confuse the word translated "authority" in this verse as the words used in other scriptures describing God-ordained authorities. This word was translated from the Greek word *katexousiazo*, which means *absolute control, domination*. It is only used twice in the New Testament. Both times it was used by Jesus (Matt. 20:25 and Mark 10:42). Jesus clearly stated this type of authority is not to be exercised in His body, the church. God is the only absolute authority. All authorities in the body of Christ are to be subject to Him and His Word. God does not give anyone in His family this type of authority, but rather, speaks against it. Matthew 20:26 **But it shall not be so among you: but whosoever will be great among you, let him be your minister;** ("minister"= *diakonos*- servant).

Jesus does not want anyone acting as though he/she has absolute control over His people. His people are subject to Him and His Word first of all, then to the persons He has placed in lesser roles of authority. However, Jesus did say there would be a "servant chief," but not "master chief." Matthew 20:27 **And whosoever will be chief among you, let him be your servant:** Believers fulfil our roles in authority by serving others as God-placed leaders, not by lording over people. His leaders are called to be servant leaders where people follow by choice, thus surrender to and strive to obey Him.

God has a great plan for your submission to your authorities. 1 Peter 2:15 **For so is the will of God, that with well doing ye may put to silence the**

ignorance of foolish men: Have you heard an unsaved person say something like: "I know people in the church who are no better than I am. They don't obey God any more than I do?" What that person was saying is, "I don't feel any responsibility to turn to God and obey Him because some believers willfully disobey His known will."

Your obedience, which is a call to submit yourself and sacrificially serve Jesus by serving His body and the unsaved in the world, sends a strong message to God and others. Your submission says "Jesus is worth serving no matter the cost." Your submission demonstrates the life transforming power of the gospel, thus gives glory to Jesus. And, a submissive attitude and life send a message that quiets rebellion. God speaks well of those who promote unity and peace. Matthew 5:9 **Blessed *are* the peacemakers: for they shall be called the children of God.**

Your good works help "**put to silence**" the arguments of unlearned men. Actions of submitting to your authorities speak more loudly for Christ than your words alone.

Someone may say, "I am free. I can do as I please." Yes, each one has the option to obey or not to obey, but disobedience always results in consequences. Freedom does not mean you can do as you please. Freedom means *you now have the liberty (freedom of choice) and power to exercise the option to do right.* Before salvation, you did not have the power to do right toward God, but in Christ you have the power to do those things which please Him, thus you are free in Him to love Him enough to do His will.

Consider your freedom in Christ as you read 1 Peter 2:16 **As free, and not using your liberty for a cloak of maliciousness, but as the servants of God. 17 Honor all men. Love the brotherhood. Fear God. Honor the king.** A "**cloak**" is an outer garment, like a large coat. It could be used to hide behind. You should not use your **liberty** in Christ to do your own will. But rather, use your freedom to make decisions to honor Him. Show Jesus you are treasuring Him by respecting authority.

No one has the right to go against God's will. However, you do have the "option" to do so, but there will be consequences if you do.

When someone in authority makes a decision that is self-serving, that is an abuse of authority. Abuse of authority is a sin and will be punished. Abuse of authority can be as damaging as rebellion to authority.

1 Peter 2:18 **Servants, be subject to your masters with all fear; not only to the good and gentle, but also to the froward.** ("**Froward**" means *perverse, crooked, bad.*) Anyone can submit to the "**good and gentle,**" but it takes faith in God to submit to the "**froward.**" However, persons with a rebellious heart will not humbly, submit to anyone, not even God. 1 Peter 2:19 **For this is thankworthy, if a man for conscience toward God endure grief, suffering wrongfully. 20 For what glory is it, if, when ye be buffeted for your faults, ye shall take it patiently? but if, when ye do well, and suffer for it, ye take it patiently, this is acceptable with God.** There is no glory to God when you suffer for doing wrong. Yet, there is great glory to Him when you patiently suffer for righteousness sake.

Romans 13:4 **For he is the minister of God to thee for good. But if thou do that which is evil, be afraid; for he beareth not the sword in vain: for he is the minister of God, a revenger to execute wrath upon him that doeth evil.** Have you thought of authorities in this country, at work, in your family, and in your church family as **ministers of God for your ultimate good**? _____ Should you humbly submit to each one for the Lord's sake?

_____ Will God reward persons who obey Him? _____ Which is best for you: having your own way or God's approval? _____

When you view your submission to authorities as gaining God's approval, you are strengthened by knowing He is pleased. Knowing you are sacrificing for Jesus gives motivation to "**endure**" suffering at the hands of corrupt or weak leaders. You can even endure suffering with joy when you know God is using those leaders to conform you to Jesus' likeness.

1 Peter 2:21 **For even hereunto were ye <u>called</u>: because Christ also <u>suffered</u> for <u>us</u>, leaving us an <u>example</u>, that ye should <u>follow</u> his steps: 22 Who did <u>no</u> sin, neither was guile found in his mouth: 23 Who, when he was reviled, <u>reviled</u> not again; when <u>he</u> suffered, he threatened not; but committed himself to <u>him</u> that judgeth righteously:** According to this passage, should one expect some suffering at the hands of authorities? ____ Did Jesus know those government authorities would have Him tortured and put to death? ____ Did Jesus fight them or submit? _____

Though he were a Son, yet learned he obedience by the things which he suffered; Hebrews 5:8

Did Jesus submit because it was easy or because it was His Father's will? _____ Jesus prayed just before His arrest, "**Father not my will but thine**." What should we pray when we don't know what to pray? We should pray for the Father's will to be done.[1] (There will be many times when a person will be unsure about how to pray). Notice how Jesus prayed when He knew He was about to be put to death. John 12:27 **Now is my soul troubled; and what shall I say? Father, save me from this hour: but for this cause came I unto this hour.** Does it seem Jesus struggled to find the right words to pray in this verse? _____ He wanted to avoid suffering if that were possible while remaining in His Father's will, but He was willing to suffer no matter the cost to please and glorify His Father. Jesus wanted His Father's approval and glory more than He wanted to live. This is the kind of desire for God that He uses to change the world. God wants to change your life and the world around you, and that, by you loving Jesus so much that, for Him, you submit to the authorities in your life.

When facing situations of submission which bring pain and suffering, pray as Jesus did, John 12:28 **<u>Father, glorify thy name</u>. Then came there a voice from heaven, saying, I have both glorified it, and will glorify it again.** The Father is committed to glorifying His Son. You are wise to join Him by striving to exalt Him in your life in every way you can. According to this verse, did Jesus glorify His Father by humble submission to His will?_____ Did submission to His Father's will also include submission to wicked, religious and government leaders? ____

If you are confused or troubled about something in your past or future and are not sure what to do, ask God to glorify His name. When you don't know what to do, pray "**Father, glorify your name in my life**" and then humbly strive to do what you understand you should.

> "In our desire after God let us always keep in mind that God has desire, and His desire is toward the sons of men who will make the once-for-all decision to exalt Him over all. Such as these are precious to God above all treasures of earth and sea. In them God finds a theater where He can display His exceeding kindness toward us in Christ Jesus. With them God can walk unhindered; toward them He can act like the God He is. In speaking thus, I have but one fear: that I may convince the mind before God can win the heart." -A. W. Tozer, Endnote 7, p. 70.

1. Are believers, at times, called to suffer in this life so God will be glorified? _____

2. List the names of some persons God has placed over you where it has been easy to submit._____

Good and wise leaders take care to be humble to make it easier for those under them to submit.

3. List the names of some where it has been or now is difficult for you to submit._____

4. Ask God to help you submit to everyone He has placed over you so He can demonstrate how thoroughly Jesus can transform one's life. By submitting yourself, you can rest assured that He is being glorified in you.

Do you get the idea this Christian life means the end to a self-centered life? _____ If so, you've got it right.

Point of Truth: We shouldn't expect a "Christian" life that is not about Christ.

5. Do you give the money God has entrusted to you to manage for Him to your local church as His Word teaches? _____ Your spending is a reflection of where your heart is.

Point of Truth: Giving is about your heart. Your giving shows God where your heart is.

The things you treasure are reflected through your spending. Does your giving show you treasure Jesus above all else? _____ Or, is there a "gap" in what you give and what you should? _____ If there is, make a firm commitment to begin to give as you know you should. Those who do not give as they should are not under God's authority. God will not make your spiritual life as fruitful as He wants if you rebel in giving as His Word teaches.

We are merely managers of all God has entrusted to us. Our attitude and spending show who we really serve (namely ourselves or God).

The battle for your heart is basically over who you will strive to live for in all areas of life. Everything boils down to your willingness to live for Jesus or for yourself. God knows your heart and He has granted to you the power to direct your heart either toward Him or toward someone or something else.

Week Six, Day Five
Subjection to Authority: God's Way to Greatness-- *a godly influence for Jesus.*
Believers Are Required to Obey the Laws of Our Land.

 Memory verse– Romans 13:1 **Let every soul be subject unto the higher powers. For there is no power but of God: the powers that be are ordained of God.**

As you study God's Word, you discover how He has ordained authorities in the earth. Words cannot express the importance of learning how vital it is to live properly related to your authorities. God will bless anyone who is careful concerning obedience in all areas of life and that certainly includes authorities.

1 Peter 2:9 **But ye are a <u>chosen</u> generation, a <u>royal</u> priesthood, an <u>holy</u> nation, a <u>peculiar</u> people; that ye should <u>show forth the praises of him</u> who hath called you out of <u>darkness</u> into his marvelous light: 10 Which in time past were not a people, but <u>are</u> <u>now</u> the people of God: which had not obtained mercy, but now have obtained mercy. 11 Dearly beloved, I beseech you as strangers and pilgrims, abstain from fleshly <u>lusts</u>, which <u>war</u> against the soul;**

You are called and being conformed to Jesus' likeness to **<u>show forth the praises of him</u> who hath called you out of <u>darkness</u> into his marvelous light:**

There will always be an ongoing war between your flesh and the Holy Spirit (See Galatians 5:17). This war takes place in your soul (your mind, will and emotions). From your heart you control who gains the victory. Whatever you strive for in your heart will be revealed by your decisions, words, attitudes and actions.

1 Peter 2:12 **Having your conversation <u>honest</u> among the Gentiles: that, whereas they speak against you as evildoers, they may by your good <u>works</u>, which they shall behold, <u>glorify</u> God in the day of visitation.**

Point of Truth: The key to submission is an overpowering desire to glorify God.

You develop an attitude of a servant to God as you become more concerned that He is pleased and glorified, rather than yourself. The passage above (1 Peter 2:9-11) reminds us of the **war** that rages inside when we seek to glorify God in all we think, say and do.

The following verses confront the flesh in a direct way. 1 Peter 2:13 **Submit yourselves to <u>every</u> ordinance of man for the Lord's <u>sake</u>: whether it be to the <u>king</u>, as supreme; 14 Or unto governors, as unto <u>them</u> that are sent by him for the punishment of evildoers, and for the praise of them that do well.** According to verse 13, for whose sake are you to submit to the laws of our land? _____ Here is an example: Do you realize when a person breaks the speed limit laws he/she is rebelling against God ordained authority? _____ Think about this: are speed limit laws there to hurt us, or to protect us? _____ Do you think each person should be able to pick and choose which law he/she will obey? _____ What if everyone sought to obey the laws of this land, would our nation be a better place to live? _____

Obeying the laws of our land (which God has ordained) is for your protection and for a better life for you. Regardless of what you have done in the past, begin to carefully obey your authorities for God's glory. Those who treasure Jesus enough to obey Him out of love have the greatest impact in the world for Him and His kingdom. They also have the most to look forward to in heaven. The faithful will be rewarded in this life and the next. You can never out give God.

To experience the things God has for you, you must strive to do all He is teaching you about being like Jesus, thus living for His glory. People strive to obey Jesus for many reasons. Yet, those who obey Him in a love-driven relationship are used to change the world. These don't need a set of rules, or some other type of outward, pressure-driven force to cause them to strive to obey. Jesus and His love constrains them. The Apostle Paul wrote of this in 2 Corinthians 5:14 **For the love of Christ constraineth us; . . .** We are kept at our post, by the love God has for us in His Son, therefore, in response, we strive to be like Him, for His glory.

We must know we cannot rear a godly generation as God wants if we pick and choose where we will obey Him. Such instability makes love appear fickle and arbitrary. This kind of relating to God confuses children and sets them up for destructive tendencies because it makes them think believers actually decide for ourselves what is right or wrong. That right only belongs to God. What is right or wrong flows out of the character and nature of God. So, right and wrong never change.

One should thank God for police officers. They are here for everyone's protection. I know they are only human, and some are corrupt, but most are not. The wrong some may do does not relieve us of our responsibility to do right.

The first verse in today's study (1 Pet. 2:9) tells how believers (God's "**Beloved**") are a different type of people, a people who seek to do right in every way so He is glorified, thus, to **show forth the praises of him**, who has called and saved us.

I know submission to authorities is not easy for some. Yet true obedience is never easy, but it always is best. As stated earlier, God's plan for your life will always have a "gap" in it. What I mean is, when God wants to do something big in your life, His call is always larger and greater than you are. At times, you will have to stretch yourself by faith to be obedient to His will. When God wants to change the world through you, He does not give you a calling (ministry or place of service) for which you are already suited. He calls you to step out and up to do what only He can do through you. We do not need God's help to do the things we can do on our own. Don't be surprised if God calls you to things that appear impossible.

" . . . Each assignment God gives is not just about His plans for history–it is itself a call to intimacy with Him.

Let me tell you something that will help you avoid burnout: The very assignment God gives a leader is a primary means through which He calls him to intimacy with Himself. It is not only what the leader does, but who the leader is, that is a picture of the reality God wants to take people toward. A leader is not just given an assignment; he becomes the portrait of the assignment.

God never separates His assignment from the sanctifying process of the leader. That's why there is always a horrendous gap between what God tells you to do and where you are. It is always way out ahead of you. . . .

This is also the reason God will never give a leader all the details of His plan. He gives him just enough to trust Him for right now. He tells him enough to let him know that he does not have all he needs, so he has to keep

> coming back to Him. The very nature of the assignments God gives us is a call to His heart.
>
> . . .
>
> Phillips Brooks, the famed New England pastor of the nineteenth century, says, 'Do not pray for tasks equal to your powers. Pray for powers equal to your tasks. Then the doing of your work shall be no miracle, but you shall be the miracle.'"[13]

Religious people, doing religious things, is not that out of the ordinary. However, you striving in surrender to Jesus out of love for Him is completely different. It shows the miracle that you are in Him.

The following passage expresses what I have tried to convey as relating to the "gap" between where we are and where God wants us to be.

1 John 3:1 **Behold, what manner of <u>love</u> the Father hath bestowed upon us, that we should be called the sons of God: therefore the world knoweth us not, because it knew him not. 2 Beloved, now are we the sons of God, <u>and it doth not yet appear what we shall be</u>: but we know that, when he shall appear, <u>we shall be like him</u>; for we shall see him as he is. 3 And every man <u>that hath this hope</u> in him <u>purifieth himself</u>, even as he is pure.**

Through this book, I have tried to help you move forward in experiencing verse three. The Greek word translated as "**hope**" means *confident expectation*, not uncertainty.

In Romans chapter 13, you are told that authorities are ordained by God as His "**ministers**" (vs. 4 & 6). When one rebels against authorities, he/she is also rebelling against God. Have you owned a radar detector? ____ If so, why? _____ Should a believer have such? ____ Should believers obey the laws? ____ You should take care to obey every law of the land (as long as the laws do not violate God's Word). Obeying the laws of the land is to be done out of love for God just like all other obedience.

We must know we **cannot** be right with God and be in rebellion against our authorities, just as a person cannot be unforgiving of others and be right with Him.

The word "**them**" in 1 Peter 2:14, refers to the officials which are sent by kings and governors. "**Them**" includes all sent by an authority. At a place of employment it refers to the administrators, supervisors, and any other positions of leadership. It refers to everyone in a capacity of authority. When an authority sends someone to you, you must treat that individual as you should treat the authority who sent him/her.

In the church, just like other places, persons in authority have been placed there by God for your good. In love-driven passion for Jesus, strive to be rightly related to all of your authorities and He will be pleased. 1 John 5:3 **For this is the <u>love of God</u>, that we keep his commandments: and his commandments are not grievous.** God has put His love in us, therefore, we strive for obedience out of love. All obedience is to be love-driven. God's commandments are not grievous,- *burdensome*, when we treasure Jesus to the point that we love Him enough to keep His commandments. As we strive to keep His commandments, because we love Him in response to His love for us, He is glorified in us.

1 John 2:5 **But whoso keepeth his word, in him verily is the love of God perfected: hereby know we that we are in him.** Assurance of salvation happens when a believer is love-driven to keep God's commandments. An unbeliever cannot keep commandments out of love for Jesus, because he/she

doesn't have a love relationship with Him. If you living in a love relationship with Jesus that is revealed by your striving to please Him because you love Him, then you can **know that** you **are in Him**.

My Journey and a Sobering Truth.

I recall an event that enhanced my approach to Bible study and learning of God's truth. Years ago, I was on my way to a training conference with a group of pastors and church leaders. As we traveled, we talked about various things. I don't recall who made the statement which God used sometime later to change my approach to obeying what I learn. Someone said, "I suppose we are going to this conference to learn something else we don't intend to do."

I didn't think much about it at the time. But later on, as I studied the material presented, I found myself at that very place. I had no intention of doing what was taught. It was okay, but not what I considered we needed to implement in the church I served.

You are in this study by choice. What are you going to do with the things God is saying to you? Obey or disobey? Circle one.

Point of Truth: You are not changed by learning truth. You are changed when you obey the truth you have learned, IF you obey out of love for Jesus, thus to see Him glorified in you.

This is why many who know a lot about the Bible are not spiritually minded. They know a lot about truth, but it is not being lived out in their lives based on love for Jesus, for His glory. Some obey out of a legal sense of obedience. This comes across as rigid and grievous.

One might ask, "How can someone know so much about the Bible and yet be so unlike Christ?" Or, "How can one know so much Biblical truth, and yet there is no anointing of God's Spirit when this one teaches or preaches?" Because merely learning truth does not bring change. Truth obeyed for the right reason brings change and that reason is love for Jesus. A person may teach truth he/she is not willing to adapt to his/her own life, and when this happens, very little change takes place. The power of God is not as active in that person as He desires. Churches have the greatest opportunity for change when their leaders live out, in love, the truth God teaches to them.

What you have studied, hopefully, has been reinforced and imparted to you by God's Spirit. Whatever He has taught to you, He expects you to apply to your life.

As I close, I am offering this prayer for everyone who studies this book. "Dear Jesus, I have sought to be as honest and open as I can. I pray I have not misunderstood your Word. Please accomplish your will in the lives of everyone who studies this book. Please bring true revival and spiritual awakening to our nation. Our only hope is YOU. Do in us the things that have been taught correctly.

Father please help me and my brothers and sisters be visible trophies of your love and grace. Help us shine brightly in love as true followers of Jesus. Help us be good examples of believers who take loving and treasuring Jesus more seriously than everything else. Help us "hold forth" the fruit that your Son is producing through us for your glory.

Again, with all that is within me, I give you my heart and all the glory, honor, and praise. I thank you for working your love in me. I love you. Amen."

If this study has helped you, please place this ministry, myself and family, on your prayer list. We can do no greater than to pray for one another. Write to us and let us know how you have been helped. You never know, your testimony might be used of God to help others.

The best thing some could do, whom God is speaking to about learning to treasure Jesus more, is to take some time alone with God in fasting, Bible study and prayer in pursuit of a closer fellowship with Jesus.

Why do you suppose God has so freely given the United States His Word, the gospel message, while at the same time made us among the richest people in the world? Could it be so we will use the wealth He has entrusted to us to take His message of salvation to the whole world?

I have written about many things that reveal the true conditions of our hearts. Giving financially through your local church for Jesus' glory is one of them. How are you sacrificially giving so others can come to know Jesus, so they can learn to treasure Him with all of their hearts for His glory? _____ _____If you are not giving as you should, there is a reason. Isn't it time to begin to give as you should? _____ If Jesus means that much to you, you will. Give to Jesus out of love in response to His love for you.

As stated, God's purpose isn't merely about the things He will accomplish through you. It is about you becoming the person He wants you to be for His Son and His glory. Your heart has everything to do with the person you will become for Jesus while on this earth. Be wise. Turn your heart to Jesus and strive with all that is within you to keep it fixed on Him and He will be glorified in you now and forever.

I wrote early in this book, "In this writing I have sought to make everything about Jesus Christ, because as the Bible teaches, everything in our lives is to be about Him. I don't fear that one day I will stand before God and hear Him say, "You took my Son too seriously. You made too much of Him." But, I do fear many will have been religious, even dedicated to His work (Matthew 7:21-23),without having a genuine, love-relationship with Him. Everyone must realize how important it is to know Him personally, to depend completely on Him, to live a love-driven life for Him.
Point of Truth: You can't make too much of Jesus, but you can make far too little of Him."

Scripture References

Genesis
6:5-6 11

Deuteronomy
30:9-10 19
32:8-9 89

1 Samuel
9:26-10:9 ... 14
13:7-14 85
13:13-14 15
15:21 86
15:24 86
15:30 87
16:7 12

2 Samuel
22:27 99

1 Kings
15:5 21

2 Chronicles
7:14 95
16:9 71

Job
1:1 82
1:9-11 82
1:16 82
1:18-19 83
1:20-22 83
9:4 82
13:15 83
17:7 37
42:7-10 83

Psalms
7:9 23
34:8 7
37:3-5 9
42:1-2 47
(57:7 Week 5
Memory Vs).
63:8 21
66:18 58
75:6-7 105
139:23-24.. 50

Proverbs
(4:23 Week 1-
Memory Vs).
(17:3 Week 2-
Memory Vs).
21:2 15

Isaiah
8:11 105
26:3 24
29:12-13 ... 30

Jeremiah
17:9 29
29:13 ... 47, 67

Malachi
3:7 100

Matthew
5:8 99
5:9 108
5:23-24 51
6:19-21 74
6:20 75
6:21 11
6:22-24 75
20:25-27 ... 107
20:26 107
21:13 58

Mark
9:29 36
9:35 107

Luke
6:27-28 77
6:45 11
6:46 60
7:1-10 96
7:8 97
7:9 97
12:33-34 ... 74
24:45-46 ... 13
24:47 35

John
1:9 75
1:12 12
8:32-36 42
14:6 12
14:20 28
14:21 ... 49, 99
14:23 49
15:5 16
15:7 57
15:7-11 16
15:9 59
15:11 51
15:11-12 ... 59
16:33 80

Acts
13:21-22 ... 21
17:24-25 39, 71
20:21 13

Romans
1:3-5 53
6:6 .... 54, 72
6:11-12 38
6:14 . 13, 45, 48, 54
8:1 68
8:26-29 56
8:28 .57, 77, 106
8:28-29 89
8:29 59
8:30 57
8:31-34 13
8:32 64
8:35-37 52
10:9-10 12
11:29 66
12:1-2 ... 8, 32
12:19 77
(13:1 Week 6
Memory Vs).
13:2 79
13:3-4 80
13:4 ...103, 108
13:5-6 104
13:7 104

1 Corinthians
9:27 77
15:9-10 54
15:24 102

2 Corinthians
1:3-10 79
3:1-18 28
3:6 29
3:15-18 45
3:17 29
3:18 30
5:14 112
10:3-5 32
12:9-10 52

Galatians
2:20 71
4:19 57

Ephesians
1:15-18 89
1:18 90
1:19 90
2:1-3 69
2:7 59
4:27 32
6:5-8 53
(6:7 Week 4-
Memory Vs).

Philippians
1:6 22
2:3-4 27
3:7-8 88
4:7 23
4:13 51

Colossians
1:9-10 91
1:10 68
1:16 40
3:1-4 65
3:16-25 48
3:23 60
(3:23 Week 3-
Memory Vs.).

1 Thessalonians
2:4 81

Hebrews
4:12 20
5:8 .... 78, 109
12:1-2 62
12:3-4 63
13:17 106

James
4:7-8 54
4:8 63

1 Peter
2:9-12 111
2:13 111
2:14 111
2:15 107
2:16-20 108
2:21-23 109

2 Peter
1:2-3 97

1 John
1:6-8 22
1:9 ...... 43, 37
2:5 113
2:6 69
2:9-10 60
2:19 66
3:1-3 113
4:16 51
4:19 63
5:3 113
5:12 13

Revelation
4:11 41

Endnotes

1. J. Edwin Orr, <u>Full Surrender</u>, (London, England; Marshall, Morgan and Scott, 1953), pp. 90-91.

2. Ibid. p. 91.

3. Institute in Basic Life Principles, <u>Life Purpose Journal</u>, Volume 3, (Oak Brook, Illinois), changes made by Larry White.

4. <u>How to Win the Heart of a Rebel</u> by Dr. S. M. Davis; Pastor of Parkmeadows Baptist Church, Linclon, Ill. By video, Institute in Basic Life Principles, Oak Brook Ill.

5. Glen Martin & Diane Ginter, <u>Drawing Closer</u>, Broadman & Holman Publishers, 1995).

6. Ronald Dunn, <u>Don't Just Stand There, Pray Something</u>, (Thomas Nelson Publishers, Nashville,   1992) p .206.

7. A. W. Tozer, <u>The Pursuit of God</u>, (Christian Publications, Inc. Camp Hill, Pennsylvania, 1982).

8. A. T. Robertson, Robertson's Word Pictures. Ephesians 1:18, (Grammatical corrections made by L. White)
www.biblestudytools.com/commentaries/robertsons-word-pictures/ephesians/ephesians-1-18.html

9. Mark Water, <u>Daily Encounters</u>, (Hendickson Publishers, Peabody, Massachusetts, 1997).

10. Charles Stanley, <u>Glorious Journey</u>, Thomas Nelson Publishers, Nashville, TN, 1996).

11. Warren W. Wiersbe, <u>The Integrity Crisis</u>, Thomas Nelson Publishers, 1991, pp. 75-76.

12. John Piper, <u>Desiring God</u>, Multnomah Publishers, Sisters, OR, 2004, p.250.

13. Crawford Loritts, <u>4 Portraits of a Leader</u>, Life Action Ministries, Volume 42, Issue 4, p. 12.

14. Watchman Nee, Spiritual Authority, Christian Fellowship Publishers, Inc, New York, 1972.

15. Oswald Chambers, <u>My Utmost for His Highest</u>, (Barbour and Comapny, Inc. Westwood, NJ, 1963).